PRAISE FOR KEISHA BLAIR'S *HOLISTIC WEALTH*

"The concept of establishing and living in alignment with a holistic wealth bank account is perhaps one of the most powerful and life changing ideas in the book."

—*Real Simple*

"Such a moving excerpt from Keisha Blair's book *Holistic Wealth*: 'Our education system teaches about linearity, not about what to do when this linear pattern breaks, not where to look for resilience, not the art of recovery from disruption.'"

—Arianna Huffington

"Everyone should read Keisha Blair's book [*Holistic Wealth*] and listen to her podcast."

—Eve Rodsky, *New York Times* bestselling author of *Fair Play* and *Find Your Unicorn Space*

"This book should be required reading! Keisha Blair spells out precisely how we can achieve holistic wealth. This is sure to help YOU find purpose and have a more meaningful, happy life."

—Dave Kerpen, *New York Times* bestselling author of *The Art of People* and chairman of Likeable Media

"None of us has as much time as we think we do—either to live for today or to plan for tomorrow. But we all have a lot to learn from Keisha Blair."

—Dr. Meg Jay, clinical psychologist, associate professor of human development at the University of Virginia, and bestselling author of *The Defining Decade* and *Supernormal*

"I loved your book [*Holistic Wealth*]. It was incredible."

—Loren Ridinger, SEVP of SHOP.COM, founder of Motives Cosmetics, and Honorary Certified Holistic Wealth™ Consultant

"Financial wellness is often sought, but its tools are rarely taught! In *Holistic Wealth,* Keisha Blair provides interesting and important insights that can help us maximize deposits and minimize withdrawals from our holistic wealth bank accounts!"

—Dr. Dinorah Nieves, PhD, a.k.a. "Dr. D," coaching consultant on the Oprah Winfrey Network's *Iyanla: Fix My Life*

"This book will make you more wealthy, but in ways that actually matter. If you live by the wisdom within these pages, it is almost a guarantee that your life will become better. Dive head-first into this book if you want to learn to overcome challenges in your life, live more deeply, and even get more out of your money and relationships. I loved this book, and I'm confident you will, too."

—Chris Bailey, international bestselling author of *Hyperfocus* and *The Productivity Project*

"Keisha Blair's book *Holistic Wealth* is full of insight and wisdom, made all the more valuable because it's been tested and refined through her unique experiences."

—Rhiannon Beaubien, managing editor of Farnam Street and *Wall Street Journal* bestselling author of The Great Mental Models series

"An amazing story of resilience."

—Amy Gallo, contributing editor for *Harvard Business Review* and author of *HBR Guide to Dealing with Conflict*

"This book is a page-turner. Really inspirational."

—Jen Rogers, award-winning anchor for Yahoo Finance's *The Final Round*

"We loved your book!"

—Amy Baczkowski, Emmy Award–winning producer, seven-time Emmy nominee, and producer of *The Mel Robbins Show*

"Using clear action-driven steps guided by the advice in many different fields, this book is a road map to living a more prosperous life. Whether you strive to be financially independent, inspire others, get healthy, or simply live the best life you possibly can, you will learn how to push past challenges and become a stronger version of yourself."

—*BELLA* magazine

"Beautiful and well-written."

—Emily C. Johnson, deputy director of editorial strategy for Thrive Global

"Keisha Blair's new book [*Holistic Wealth*] . . . makes prosperity look inviting and accessible."

—KJ Dell Antonia, *New York Times* bestselling author of *The Chicken Sisters* and *How to Be a Happier Parent* and former editor of "Well Family" at the *New York Times*

"There is a little gem of wisdom on almost every page of this book. Nice work, Keisha Blair!"

—Anne Dimon, editor-in-chief of *Travel to Wellness* and president of the Wellness Tourism Association

"Absolutely everyone needs to take the time to slow down, breathe, and reorient yourself, but especially women dealing with trauma or change. *Holistic Wealth* will help you focus on rebuilding and reemerging into the world, on your terms."

—Holly Lörincz, bestselling author of *Crown Heights*

"This book is about financial independence and so much more. Keisha Blair has a very powerful story, and people can really identify with [it]. I think many people can really use this story to help with what we have gone through [with COVID]. It's a great book."

—Emma Chapman, co-founder of A Beautiful Mess

"Deliciously inviting."

—Malena Crawford, bestselling author of *A Fistful of Honey* and Certified Holistic Wealth™ Consultant

OTHER BOOKS BY KEISHA BLAIR

Holistic Wealth: 32 Life Lessons to Help You Find Purpose, Prosperity, and Happiness

Holistic Wealth Personal Workbook

HOLISTIC WEALTH

EXPANDED AND UPDATED

HOLISTIC WEALTH

EXPANDED AND UPDATED

36 LIFE LESSONS to Help You Recover from DISRUPTION, Find Your LIFE PURPOSE, and Achieve FINANCIAL FREEDOM

KEISHA BLAIR

FOREWORD BY
KELLY RUTHERFORD

GIRL FRIDAY BOOKS

Published by Girl Friday Books™, Seattle
www.girlfridaybooks.com

Produced by Girl Friday Productions

Cover design by Mumtaz Mustafa and Paul Barrett
Image credits: Cover sparkle image © Shutterstock, Chinnapong

ISBN (paperback): 978-1-954854-36-9
ISBN (e-book): 978-1-954854-37-6

Quote from Oprah Winfrey's commencement address on May 11, 2018, at the University of Southern California's Annenberg School for Communication and Journalism, has been quoted with the permission of Harpo, Inc. and is licensed for the purposes of this book. Excerpt of the *New Yorker* article "Six Degrees of Lois Weisberg" that appeared in the print edition of the January 11, 1999, issue, is quoted with the permission of Malcolm Gladwell. Story with Dave Kerpen and Senator Frank Lautenberg retold with the permission of Dave Kerpen. Excerpt from article "9 Signs You Fear Taking Calculated Risks" used by permission of author Amy Morin. Quote from "What to Do When a Personal Crisis Is Hurting Your Professional Life," published by the *Harvard Business Review*, used with permission from Amy Gallo. Quotes from Deepak Chopra have been used with the permission of Deepak Chopra, LLC. Kimberly Foss has been quoted with the author's permission. Quote from *The Science of Awe* by permission of Summer E. Allen, PhD. Quote from *The Top Five Regrets of the Dying* (Hay House) by permission of Bronnie Ware. Meg Jay has been quoted with the author's permission. Ellen Langer has been quoted with the author's permission. Bill T. Jones has been quoted with the author's permission.

19 20 21 22 5 4 3 2 1

Library of Congress Control Number: 2021921968

First edition

To the most important people in my life, who were the first examples and helped me to achieve holistic wealth. My children, Matthew, Alex, and Ella, my most precious assets, who have filled my holistic wealth bank account with love. To my mom, Dr. Bernice Williams, and my husband, Lindsay Blair, thank you.

In loving memory of Garfield R. Mullings, MSc, CGA, CPA

CONTENTS

PART III: PHYSICAL AND SPIRITUAL NOURISHMENT

PART IV: GOODWILL AND STRONG RELATIONSHIPS

PART V: APPLYING HOLISTIC WEALTH

FOREWORD

A BRIEF INTERVIEW WITH ACTRESS KELLY RUTHERFORD

Author's note: I met Kelly Rutherford after an introduction by mutual friends, and Kelly appeared on the Holistic Wealth Podcast with Keisha Blair *to discuss her personal journey. For context, Kelly endured a very painful and public custody battle for her two children. But even in the face of adversity, Kelly used her strength and gratitude to emerge victorious in her life. What follows is a portion of the interview as well as Kelly's written thoughts on using* Holistic Wealth *as a framework to help you master disruption.*

Keisha Blair: In this book, as you know, I tell the story of how I was widowed at a young age, just eight weeks after giving birth to my second child. I have a line about the art of recovery from disruption, and it's talking about how we get over these life-altering setbacks. I feel like you've mastered that art. You've overcome some significant challenges and taken the view that your life is so much greater in terms of your impact on humanity than any one struggle or any one challenge. For those of us who have been through those types of setbacks, I think that's the point we reach eventually after we've gone through the challenges and the pain and the grief. Can you talk a bit about how you overcame those challenges that you faced in your own life, especially with what happened with your kids? For a mother, that must have been the most painful thing. So, I'm just wondering if you can tell us a bit of what that process was like for you and how you came through that.

Kelly Rutherford: I think a lot of it is focus. First there is the shock of it to overcome. And by shock, I am talking about the setback or disruption. I think shock is what most of us feel initially. At least that's what I felt. That it was even possible that it could even happen to me was just so beyond my scope of belief, which I think is what most of us feel in the moment when something so disruptive is happening. And this makes us feel so out of control with whatever it is, whether it's our health or whether it's personal—our family, our finances—and so once I was over the initial shock, then, well, my heart broke.

And when you have your heart broken, in any capacity, it takes time to recover and heal.

What helped me a lot was getting over any blame or dwelling in feelings of victimhood. Those two emotional states are what keep us stuck, or what were keeping me stuck. I was feeling like I was a victim of this situation or the system or whatever it was, and looking for someone or something to blame. And that wasn't productive, even if I was justified on both counts. I mean, nobody would have argued with me if I said I'm blaming these people and I'm a victim of this situation. But, for me personally, the only thing that started to make sense was: How do I get my power back as a human being, as just a person? And how can I be there for my children?

I mean, it became about love and empowering myself with another mindset that wasn't looking for someone to blame and/or seeing myself in the victim role. It was like, "Well, what does that look like?" And most of that came from the energy of love, which is why I talk about it so much, because it's the most healing energy that I know of that I've found. It just became about love. Look, I love my kids, and however I can show up for them, I will. Even if I show up and I'm a mess, and I'm crying, or I show up and I have two dollars in my pocket, or I show up and I'm not sure. You just have to keep showing up and letting them know that all you want is to show up for them, the best way you can. I think that when you're honest, they receive it differently. And I was able to be honest with them; I was able to be emotionally honest.

I would ask them, how can I be the best mom for you? How can I, under these circumstances, be the best for you? And it became about staying healthy, so that when this, at some point, is hopefully resolved, I'm going to be healthy mentally, physically, and spiritually for my children so that I can watch them grow up. So these all became factors in my recovery from disruption. I found that you almost have to step away from it first. And that doesn't mean you don't have your pity parties, which are justified, it just means that most of the time you're thinking: Okay, what can I be grateful for? What can I be grateful for in all of this? What can I appreciate in all of this? What can I look for that's good? And that's when things started to shift, too—when I stopped resisting it, and fighting it, and going up against it, and looking at all the bad stuff that I felt was going on. That's when I was able to refocus. I wouldn't allow myself to talk about it anymore, either. And that started changing things, too. Or when I did talk about it, I talked about anything I could find that was an upside or a positive.

There's room for mistakes. We're all fumbling and figuring it out. None of us are going to have all the answers or say it right all the time, or do it right all the time, but the more we all acknowledge when we do make mistakes, things get better, and we rise together. So we're now given this time [during COVID-19] to realize how much we are going to need each other going forward—that's becoming golden. People are coming from an authentic place, and a loving place, and it's about money, yes, but if we're doing what we love, and finding things we love, and connecting with what we love, we prosper, and when we all do this, we all win.

***

A FINAL NOTE FROM KELLY

Keisha Blair's game-changing book, *Holistic Wealth,* allows us to find courage to overcome fear and setbacks, strengthening our connections to the world. Now, more than ever, it's important to cultivate feelings of self-worth, love, and acceptance for ourselves and others—even in the midst of setbacks. A new way forward means we can't hold on to a victim mindset, but must instead choose a holistic wealth mindset that enriches us. By finding our purpose and passions in doing what we love, and connecting with the people and things we love, then we prosper. *Holistic Wealth* is indeed the framework for the art of recovery from disruption.

—Kelly Rutherford, actress, philanthropist, entrepreneur, and Honorary Certified Holistic Wealth™ Consultant

INTRODUCTION

The global pandemic has been dubbed the greatest disruption since World War II. Living with the consequences of massive personal upheaval will be the norm for the millions of children and adults who have lived through COVID-19. However, this wasn't my family's first storm. My husband's tragic and untimely death eight weeks after I gave birth was.

A sudden, unanticipated death has a way of jolting us to our senses. When you're told that your husband is dead, everything changes in an instant. Life as you know it will never be the same—even though it can be reinvented and reshaped into something different. How we re-form our lives after tremendous disruption determines our future. Individually, it affects our families and our closest loved ones. And collectively? It can change the trajectory of humanity.

Human beings have always encountered tremendous adversity. Like our planet's relationship with Mother Nature, we are faced with our own personal hurricanes and tornadoes that lift fragments of our precious lives and scatter the bits and pieces. We wonder if it's possible to pick up those pieces and put them back together. This is the epitome of chaos, something that feels decidedly masculine to me, while order seems rather feminine. My life is a testament to the truth that we can overcome the chaos of adversity. I am a maternal near-miss survivor—I nearly died in childbirth with my first child. Three years later my husband, Garfield, died suddenly and unexpectedly just eight weeks after I gave birth to my second child. Then years later, COVID-19 hit.

For my family, the tragedies of my husband's death and COVID-19 were eerily similar in speed and impact. The sense of uncertainty at the beginning of the pandemic brought me back in time to my husband's illness—most doctors had never seen a living case of the disease my husband had. With COVID-19, many doctors had only read about pandemics in textbooks. Now, globally, we were all trying to learn how to approach a terrifying new reality. With everyone facing a massive personal disruption at the same time, I realized that the lessons I had learned after my husband's death were more important than ever.

When I published an article on Arianna Huffington's Thrive Global about the forty life lessons I learned after my husband's death, I never dreamed it would go viral. I simply published it and left it. But I knew one thing—it was the most vulnerable piece of writing I had ever created. I bared so much in that article that I was terrified. But I wanted to help. I wanted particularly to let all women know that after facing difficulties big and small you *can* make a comeback and live the life you really want.

The editorial team at Medium.com contacted me to create an audio version as part of a series of their favorite stories. "My Husband Died at Age 34; Here Are 40 Life Lessons I Learned from It"[1] was featured on or linked to by over 160 websites and viewed by more than fifty million people all over the world. It hit number one on Google for the search term

---

1. Keisha Blair, "My Husband Died at Age 34. Here Are 40 Life Lessons I Learned from It," Medium, December 13, 2017, https://medium.com/thrive-global/my-husband-died-at-age-34-here-are-40-life-lessons-ive-learn-t-17b102935efe.

"my husband died," and it is still number one at the time of writing this book. Thibaut Buccellato, award-winning French filmmaker, then contacted me to collaborate on a short film titled *The Moments I Miss*, which was filmed in Paris. I wrote the script for the short film, which was based on my experience with grief, and I was portrayed in the film by Australian actress and model Bambi Northwood-Blyth, who has graced the covers of *Vogue Japan*, *Marie Claire Italy*, and *V* magazine, just to name a few.

The traditional concept of "wealth," as defined solely by a person's net income and material possessions, needs to be revised by a whole new generation of women who value not just amassing physical assets but also collecting experiences, engaging in meaningful work, and having more control over their time. It's the hour for women to become advocates for a new concept of wealth that includes health and well-being and a life well lived. I want all women to join me in the movement for a new concept of holistic wealth.

Aristotle spoke about the "art of wealth-getting" and the need for riches to be measured by more than just acquisition of money. He states, "Originating in the use of coin, the art of getting wealth is generally thought to be chiefly concerned with it, and to be the art which produces riches and wealth; having to consider how they may be accumulated . . . Hence men seek after a better notion of riches and of the art of getting wealth than the mere acquisition of the coin, and they are right."[2]

Holistic wealth incorporates mindfulness into our everyday lives; it includes experiences and time for nonmaterial pursuits. Millennials and Gen Xers are embracing this trend and are naming sabbaticals or increased travel as financial goals—things that would never have been identified with

2. Aristotle, *Politica*, Book 1, Parts I–II, 1127–1130, http://web.archive.org/web/20080829221338/http:/etext.lib.virginia.edu/toc/modeng/public/AriPoli.html.

financial goals in the past. It is indeed a new framework, and it can be used within organizations to define and evaluate policies related to employee well-being, as well as society writ large, including governmental, nonprofit, and international development organizations. I will call that framework a Holistic Wealth Development Index, which can be used to assess human development from the perspective of fostering the art of recovery from disruption, resilience, and the ability to bounce back from life-altering setbacks.

Each of us also makes decisions that act as deposits to or withdrawals from our holistic wealth bank account. It is imperative that we think about our actions and decisions as adding or depleting our holistic wealth. If you apply this approach—the Holistic Wealth Method—to your decision-making by thinking first whether an act represents a "deposit" to or a "withdrawal" from your holistic wealth bank account, your life will never be the same, and you will be on your way to achieving holistic wealth. This can be life transforming—and leads to a whole new change in mindset: the Holistic Wealth Mindset, with decision-making based on deposits to or withdrawals from your holistic wealth bank account.

These decisions also create holistic wealth ripple effects in our lives and can affect the holistic wealth of future generations. However, it is also imperative that society as a whole enables individuals to make these choices that add to holistic wealth through application of the Holistic Wealth Development Index.

THE ART OF HOLISTIC WEALTH

For the purposes of this book, I have defined *holistic wealth* as a broad term. It refers to wealth that comprises various elements—financial savvy and independence, a life purpose and mission, spiritual connection, and a generous demeanor—all of which lead to a greater sense of wholeness and resilience in times of difficulty, and to happiness and joy. At a basic level, holistic wealth emphasizes wealth in key aspects of life, including financial wealth; physical health, emotional and spiritual wealth; and wealth in our relationships with others as well as in our contributions to humanity. These elements are interdependent, and they are necessary building blocks. Abundance in these key areas strengthens wealth in others. We might be able to hold on to financial wealth in the long term even if we don't have emotional and physical health, but its value will be very little without these other important ingredients.

Cultivating holistic wealth helps us to be mentally tough and to have *grit* to weather the inevitable storms and setbacks that life brings. We are creatures of habit, and we often operate mindlessly, making the same decisions repeatedly, sometimes to our detriment, until we experience a shock to the system. This shock makes us aware of the fact that we need to be more strategic about our daily decisions. This is no mean feat, given that the average person makes over thirty-five thousand decisions every day.[3] If we react to disruptions fearfully or habitually, or even nonstrategically, then it's almost impossible to achieve holistic wealth. We also need to be intentional in our pursuit of holistic wealth. We need a skillfully planned schema or a road map that gets us to the purpose. We need to look at our resources and constraints and figure out where the gaps are, and then go after the resources we need to meet our goals. That's why I also coined the term *holistic wealth bank account*—referred to several times in this book—to include

---

3. Eva M. Krockow, "How Many Decisions Do We Make Each Day?" *Psychology Today*, September 27, 2018, https://www.psychologytoday.com/ca/blog/stretching-theory/201809/how-many-decisions-do-we-make-each-day.

actions that can either fill or represent a withdrawal from that bank account.

MOTIVATION FROM WITHIN

This book is a culmination of life lessons that became evident to me during my own process of healing as I was on the path to where I am today. Taking an executive leadership training course at Harvard University also opened my eyes to holistic wealth and creating an intentionally designed life. Through a series of tactics and strategic moves, some of the greatest leaders of all time achieved success. Theirs wasn't mindless decision-making; they made a series of deliberate steps designed to make revolutionary change. They had goals bigger than any job title or paycheck. They had *big, bold dreams.* They had, at minimum, a vision and a mission. This book is also based on a framework I call Motivation from Within (MFW) that encompasses six laws for life. These timeless laws govern all of creation and have been an integral part of our existence. Some of these laws, like the Law of Abundance, have biblical origins, and we are therefore building on old ideas that have universal applications:

Law #1: The Law of Abundance
Law #2: Spiritual Self-Renewal
Law #3: Purpose in Life (Service to Humanity)
Law #4: The Law of Reciprocity
Law #5: The Law of Natural Harmony and Balance
Law #6: The Law of Continuous Learning

All of life's lessons relate to the universal laws, are interdependent, and form a feedback loop geared to increasing personal growth and success. Our spiritual, physical, mental, and emotional states are highly intertwined. Letting go of limiting beliefs that lead to depression, procrastination, and mindlessness is critical. The more focused you are in pursuing spiritual self-renewal and in setting the direction of progress in your life, the more effectively you can exercise personal leadership and management. And spiritual self-renewal forms the nucleus that brings forth our purpose.

As you become involved in lifelong learning, you increase your knowledge and capacity for growth and career transitions. Travel is one of the best forms of education and, from the viewpoint of holistic wealth, usefully adds to learning that takes place outside the classroom.

Another fundamental lesson is that financial security does not lie in your salary alone; it includes your ability to leverage your financial resources to produce more—through long-term investments and taking measured risks.

Holistic wealth involves growing into a better version of ourselves. If we can identify and name our "dry bones"—negative feelings such as fear, worry, frustration, doubt, anger, and regret that come from our struggles, tragedies, and setbacks—while understanding that we can determine our path forward, then we can utterly change our trajectory and set the direction of progress in our own lives.

Your circumstances, your past choices, who you were back then, and even how people wish you to be now need not define you. When I first became a widow, some people said to me, "Oh, you can't do this because you don't have a husband" and "You can't do that because it's one salary now, and you have two kids to feed." This is why I take female economic empowerment very seriously. When society gives women these messages, it's tantamount to saying, "You will never be enough." I want all women to know that we *are* enough, it's useless comparing ourselves with others, and that we have the power to flip the script.

Having spent my career working in various capacities as a senior economic adviser, including for the federal government, I've had the opportunity to explore women's economic issues in my professional life and in the personal volunteer initiatives I've established.

I started my career working on World Bank projects and also working on economic development projects sponsored by the Inter-American Development Bank. I've also worked on projects such as public sector budgeting from an international comparative perspective commissioned by the Organisation for Economic Co-operation and Development (OECD). I was a senior economist working on writing aspects of the federal budget in areas such as innovation, regional development, and economic growth. I was part of the prime minister's supporting delegation to the World Economic Forum in Davos, Switzerland, in 2018, as well as the thirteenth annual East Asia Summit in Singapore. I also worked on the Fortune Global Forum in Toronto, which brought together some of the world's most powerful business leaders and CEOs, as well as on the Fortune Most Powerful Women Summit in Montreal.

Because I also wanted to also provide mentorship and scholarships for students, I set up a nonprofit website with free resources (www.Aspire-Canada.com) and established a memorial scholarship fund in memory of my husband (the Aspire-Canada Scholarship) for youth in university. Due to reader response from the first edition of this book, I set up the Institute on Holistic Wealth (www.instituteonholisticwealth.com), with resources and online courses.

I also set up a website called the Modern Widow (www.themodernwidow.com) to provide young widows with advice on juggling a career and parenting so they can thrive and grow. Due to reader demand, I've also included one-on-one coaching on my site www.keishablair.com. I've covered a whole range of topics on these platforms, but ultimately the purpose of my endeavors boils down to one thing: I've found a higher purpose through grief and tragedy, and I want to share this purpose with you.

For this book, I've interviewed more than one hundred trailblazers, influencers, and celebrities who are world-renowned experts in these life lessons, such as Dr. Dinorah Nieves, a.k.a. "Dr. D," the coaching consultant on the Oprah Winfrey Network's *Iyanla: Fix My Life*; Tia-Clair Toomey, widely regarded as the "fittest woman on earth"; Dr. Gail Saltz, clinical associate professor of psychiatry at Weill Cornell Medicine and sister of Nobel Prize–winning astrophysicist Adam Riess; Apryl Jones from the reality TV show *Love & Hip Hop: Hollywood*; Osric Chau, Canadian actor and martial artist, best known for his role as Kevin Tran in the CW series *Supernatural* and as Vogel in the BBC America series *Dirk Gently's Holistic Detective Agency*; Dr. Robert R. Johnson, CFA, CAIA, professor of finance at Creighton University and coauthor of *Strategic Value Investing*, a book that has been on Warren Buffett's Berkshire Hathaway annual meeting reading list for the past four years; and many others. I have also drawn on fields such as philosophy, history, psychology, economics, neuroscience, and religion.

THE ART OF RECOVERY FROM DISRUPTION

As a result of the publication of the first edition of this book, we now have a global movement for holistic wealth. During COVID-19, I had many individuals reach out to me personally, wanting to know how to figure out their personal financial identities (a core concept that I discuss in detail in Part II of this book). Readers began requesting a certification program for offering financial advice, targeted to women, based on the book. They cited the tremendous importance of women's economic security, as well as the gaps in the financial advice provided to women that I had highlighted in the first edition of the book. From my experience, I knew this was a global problem. Women weren't being adequately served with tailored financial advice, the advice they were getting wasn't holistic enough, and it did not align well with many women's values of a life well lived—or with the need for more control over their time and money. COVID-19 has exacerbated these inequities and disparities.

I took those requests seriously, and I developed the Certified Holistic Wealth™ Consultant Program during the first few months of the pandemic. I also set up the Keisha Blair Institute on Holistic Wealth. Now we are building an army of certified consultants who are training women to develop their own Holistic Wealth Portfolios all over the globe (come join us!)—and some of these consultants are giving free workshops for adults and teens on holistic wealth and financial literacy. We also have Honorary Certified Holistic Wealth™ Consultants, who have impacted women all over the world with their charity work and through their professional and business endeavors. These trailblazers include iconic Hollywood actress Kelly Rutherford (author of this book's foreword, and star of several hit TV series such as *Gossip Girl*, *Melrose Place*, and *Dynasty*) as well as Loren Ridinger, SEVP of Market America and SHOP.COM and founder of Motives Cosmetics. Combined, our Honorary Certified Holistic Wealth™ Consultants have reached more than fifty million people globally with their platforms, including workshops and entrepreneurial endeavors, as well as charity work around the world.

On the *Holistic Wealth Podcast with Keisha Blair*, launched during COVID-19, I've interviewed many female entrepreneurs and influencers, and we have listeners who tuned in during the pandemic from more than fifteen countries including Canada,

Jamaica, and Mexico. The podcast has made an appearance in the Top 50 Apple Podcasts in the business category.

During the pandemic, we experienced unprecedented disruption on a scale and magnitude most of us had never seen before, and my own personal history of disruption expanded along with it. I had family members who died from COVID; others became seriously injured as a result of its effects. I experienced a back injury during the first half of lockdown, my body sending me a message that the pace I was living at was no longer sustainable. It forced me to listen. It forced me to slow down. Prior to the pandemic, I had the opportunity to support Canada's supporting delegation in the area of foreign direct investment. As the first Black woman on the supporting delegation (and, often, the only Black woman in the room), I placed tremendous weight on myself. In order to leave no room for error, to represent generations before me and after me, I put psychological pressure on myself to properly "represent" (like many Black women in this position). My back bore the cumulative weight of years of personal pressure—and so in some ways, I was not surprised when it finally cracked.

It dawned on me that this message of holistic wealth, which had gained even more devotees during the pandemic, had become more significant now than ever before. But in addition to teaching readers how to build wealth on a holistic level, I felt I needed to further focus on the art of recovery from disruption. We live in an age of disruption. How we respond day-by-day determines our overall success, and this includes applying a holistic wealth lens to our decisions (e.g., the Holistic Wealth Method), and having all the right tools in our toolbox (e.g., our Holistic Wealth Portfolios).

The pandemic has helped people define what they really value and what success means to them. During COVID-19 we were faced with our personal and collective mortality on a daily basis. This reality forced us to change priorities and look at what's important in a new way. People are not willing to accept the same burnout and stress in their lives that they once accepted. As our collective life expectancy suffered its biggest drop since World War II due to COVID-19 (according to a new study published in the *BMJ*)[4]—and for Black and Hispanic people, that decline in life expectancy was by an average of three years[5]—it became clearer that our physical health and wealth are highly intertwined. Blacks and Latinos have also faced disproportionate economic and health impacts from COVID-19, as outlined by the Center for American Progress. When life expectancy is cut short, then the losses in wealth expand exponentially over generations.

We're also starting to think about the parts of our pandemic lives that we want to take into our post-pandemic future. People are starting to redefine success on their own terms. We are seeing a new generation—I call them the Holistic Wealth Generation—rise up. After tragedy and life-altering events, people begin to realize that they don't want to define themselves only in terms of their résumés and a title bestowed upon them by an employer. This is especially so for minority women—who face frequent barriers in the workplace and systemic discrimination. During COVID-19, we witnessed historical upheavals and racial tensions in the wake of George Floyd's murder and the massive protests that followed. The Black community in particular experienced unprecedented levels of trauma due to both COVID-19 and racially motivated

---

4. Allison Aubrey, "The Pandemic Led to the Biggest Drop in U.S. Life Expectancy since WWII, Study Finds," NPR, June 23, 2021, https://www.npr.org/2021/06/23/1009611699/the-pandemic-led-to-the-biggest-drop-in-u-s-life-expectancy-since-ww-ii-study-fi.
5. Julie Bosman, Sophie Kasakove, and Daniel Victor, "U.S. Life Expectancy Plunged in 2020, Especially for Black and Hispanic Americans," *New York Times*, July 21, 2021, https://www.nytimes.com/2021/07/21/us/american-life-expectancy-report.html.

violence. What we're seeing now is a shift toward a life based on a more fulfilling, sustainable definition of success—one which also includes well-being, social justice for all, being able to tap into inner peace and joy, and having the time to engage in more meaningful experiences.

In a post-pandemic world, the onus is on employers to provide more support to their employees in terms of well-being and mental and emotional health. Instead of chasing productivity targets, we need to incorporate well-being and recharging practices into our day-to-day lives. We also need diversity initiatives, which can be very effective at addressing issues faced by Black women in particular, who are victims of frequent microaggressions and are often micromanaged at work. The next step is to embed holistic wealth practices into the daily fabric of work and home, with the relevant tools—remembering that holistic wealth also includes social justice and using your power and platform to stomp out hate and racism—in order to lower stress and burnout.

The truly unexpected response to the first edition of the book, and the global impact of the pandemic, gave me the courage to expand the lessons to include more about the art of recovery from disruption, to explore more deeply things like how we can develop the assets that truly sustain us through life's inevitable suffering and heartache, what lends us resilience when we face hard times, and what allows us to renew ourselves after a setback so we can keep moving forward as we forge the life we want—even if it doesn't look the way we once thought it would. This book is a culmination of what I've learned as a result of struggle and grief. It is also a methodical guide to the life lessons that helped me get past those times and to resources that encompass so much more than simple finances, though these are an integral part of the equation. It's an approach to well-being through and after calamity. It's *holistic wealth.*

More than anything, I hope learning about holistic wealth will encourage you. I hope you find the ideas helpful. I hope that you know, above all else, that your life is a sweet gift—that you can use it to become anything you want to, and for the larger benefit of humanity. And if you are in the middle of obstacles now or if they come your way, I hope you refer to this guide and remember that the greatest power lies within you. I wish you holistic wealth in every aspect of your life.

Love, Keisha

PART I

INTENTIONAL LIFE PURPOSE

1

LIFE, WELL LIVED

Life, if well lived, is long enough.

—Lucius Annaeus Seneca

I have never seen a tumor so big in a person so young in all my medical practice," the investigative coroner said to me over the phone.

Dr. Gordon Watt had been assigned to my husband's case; they had just completed the autopsy, but it was still inconclusive. They knew it was a tumor and they knew it was the size of a grapefruit, but they didn't know what type or the origin. This became a medical investigation, and they had to send it to the United States for testing. A regional and international team of doctors and pathologists had to be assembled to examine the case. It took one year for those autopsy results. My husband, Garfield, had a disease that only one in a million people get each year. The disease is so rare that most doctors will never see it in their lifetime—they can only read about it in textbooks. As Dr. Watt told me years later, "It's one of those illnesses you get taught in medical school—but most doctors never encounter it."

My husband died not knowing he had this disease. At that point, we had been married for only seven years. Matthew Ricardo was three years old, and Alexander Benjamin was born just eight weeks prior to Garfield's death.

Garfield didn't realize it was his last day on earth when he arose on the morning of April 8. He didn't know he was ill with a lethal disease. Merely to get a medical diagnosis, the odds were stacked against him. He didn't know he would have only three hours from the time he arrived at the emergency room to the moment they would call the time of his death. And he didn't know that during those three hours, the doctors didn't stand a chance of finding the tumor, much less arresting its growth. He didn't know he had an illness most doctors don't know to look or test for, an illness only found during autopsies in 70 percent of cases. He didn't know that despite medical and technological advancement, he stood no chance against this lethal enemy.

I didn't know that this was the last three hours I would spend with him, while the doctors, puzzled and confused, lifted their hands in sheer surrender.

Most of us don't realize how little time we have to live. We think we have endless days or years to make changes. We think we're young and invincible, that our life cycle will follow a certain musical structure and rhythm, a set of rules and patterns around which we can plan and create a family. We depend on that rhythmic structure—a delicate balance of stressed and unstressed beats in an orchestral performance—to bring meaning to the cycle of life. We are educated in these rhythms.

Children are born to two loving parents who rear them into loving adults who then procreate and then have grandchildren, and so forth. We are used to a system of procreation and ancestry that preserves our history, culture, and memory—certain syncretized elements that hold the compositional patterns of our family, such as our genetic makeup, or voice and hair. Ancient systems of classifications were put forward based on linearity and direction. Time and the seasons move in a linear fashion. We have come to expect a pattern—within the context of weather patterns, culture, history, and preservation of our heritage.

So it is with the life cycle and families. Some of us can trace our family heritage as Scottish or British Highlanders. Some of us can trace our family lineage from slavery. We can track our ancestors' march across the world toward modernity—just like the game of chess, with its very humble beginnings as *chaturanga* in India, so it is that our ancestors' evolution can be traced. Our entire evolution and history are tied to sociological and economic events. When the life cycle is disrupted, all these elements break down and the losses become generational.

Some of us never think we have but a week, a month, a year to live. Even if we are diagnosed with an illness, we assume we will have time to "buy more time" and "fight the good fight." We never think it will be quick, fierce, and lethal. We never think that our soul—the very essence of who we are—will depart from our earthly bodies so quickly, leaving a vacant box for our families to peer upon.

When they called Garfield's time of death, I stood surrounded by a sea of doctors in blue scrubs and gazed over at the flatlined heart monitor, knowing his soul was still there. I stroked his fingers, and they were soft and warm. He could still hear me then. But by the time they brought his personal effects in the white plastic bag, and once they laid the white cotton sheet across his body, his soul had already left. The essence of my husband was gone, and the body was now an empty vessel. What lay before me was a container for burial. Death lay across his face. I knew in an instant—we had now lost him forever.

* * *

Ancient Egyptians believed that the *ka* (the most vital part of the soul) was bestowed upon individuals at birth by Heket or Meskhenet, who breathed this "energy" into their lungs for their first breath. They believed that, upon death, the *ka* left the body, passing to the afterlife and marking the difference between the living and the dead. Call it a soul or *ka*—the essence of my husband was gone.

Legend has it that Henry Ford was convinced that the soul of a person was located in the last breath, and so he captured the last breath of his best friend and idol, Thomas Edison, in a test tube. I could not capture Garfield's voice for my sons to listen to in the future. Years later, when Alexander—whose father had died eight weeks after his birth—asked me if I remembered what Garfield's voice sounded like, I recalled the missing links in a chain that are forever lost when the linear life cycle is disrupted. I can still hear Garfield's voice and have captured it in my brain and heart in sacred vessels, but for Alexander, that voice is gone forever. For me, the death of a husband was devastating, but for Alexander and Matthew, a part of their history died, and for this there was no replacement.

The lesson is obvious, and we say it often, but I don't think most of us have really let it soak in: *Life is short. It is gone in the blink of an eye.*

When I found myself widowed at age thirty-one, eight weeks after I gave birth to my second child, I thought, "You have got to be kidding me! We were both supposed to be outlived by our two-month-old baby." *Not so.* This did not happen.

Instead, I was burying my husband. I was convinced I was in a dream for months afterward. In this state, I began to deeply question everything.

Had I been living life like I really meant it? No, I hadn't. I hadn't been authentically who I wanted to be. I had been a new mom and overwhelmed with life, trying to juggle a career and two babies. I hardly had time to spend with friends. To say I had been overwhelmed was an understatement. I had given up on hobbies and the things I loved because I felt like I had no choice. It was the only way I knew how to make it work.

Flash forward to the white plastic bag of Garfield's belongings. Within the blink of an eye, my whole outlook changed. I walked into the hospital emergency room with my husband living and breathing and walked out three hours later without a husband, only a white plastic bag in my hand. I went home and put away the smaller items—the jewelry, including his wedding ring, his watch, and a bracelet—to give to the boys one day. Garfield wore these items when he drew his last breath, and this was all they would have of their father.

Before they gave me the bag and before they performed resuscitation, I prayed that God would give me a second chance with him. I prayed that he'd survive this ordeal. As nurses shuttled past me with bags full of blood to give him, and a din of activity swirled around me, I tried bargaining with God, saying I would do anything, give up anything, if he only survived. Those prayers weren't answered. Sometimes the bargaining doesn't work. In the final hours and minutes of life, when the cosmos has shifted, we don't get a repeat, a rewind, or a do-over.

On his last day, when Garfield called me from work, he sounded tired and stressed. If we had known this day was to be his last, we would have spent it together. For years afterward, I wished I could have back that day, and the months leading up to it, so we could make the most of every moment.

In the months that followed Garfield's death, I realized I needed to live life on my terms, doing the things that brought me real happiness and joy. The only chance we have is the here and now. You have today, and you will likely have tomorrow, to live like you mean it. Don't wait for an unspecified time in the future to do "it." Don't wait until you have to bargain and negotiate for something that is entirely out of your control.

Danish philosopher and theologian Søren Kierkegaard maintained that the individual is solely responsible for giving her own life meaning and for living passionately and sincerely, in spite of obstacles including trauma, tragedy, despair, angst, absurdity, and alienation. In *Thoughts on Crucial Situations in Human Life: Three Discourses on Imagined Occasions*, published in 1845 (translated by David F. Swenson in 1941), he writes the following:

> *The Storm: Is Knowledge Changed When It Is Applied?*
>
> Let us imagine a pilot, and assume that he had passed every examination with distinction, but that he had not as yet been at sea. Imagine him in a storm; he knows everything he ought to do, but he has not known before how terror hits the seafarer when the stars are lost in the blackness of the night; he has not known the sense of impotence that comes when the pilot sees the wheel in his hand become a plaything for the waves; he has not known how the blood rushes to the head when one tries to make calculations at such a moment; in short, he has had no conception of the change that takes place in the knower when he has to apply his knowledge.

This passage could also be describing the terror of death. What will you do when death comes and sits on your bed and then lies down beside you? What will you do when death's sting takes over in the final moments of your life? Will you have regrets?

Our education system teaches about linearity, not about what to do when this linear pattern breaks, not where to look for resilience, not the art of recovery from disruption. Knowledge that you are living your life well is a resource you can draw on well into your final hours. Consider the questions asked by acclaimed author, choreographer, and director Bill T. Jones, who was awarded the National Medal of Arts in 2014 by President Barack Obama. He choreographed a dance and later gave his memoir the same title, *Last Night on Earth,* based on the loss of his partner to AIDS. In the dance he speaks to the audience directly from the stage: "What time is it? . . . Can you at this moment look in the mirror and be all right with it? . . . Are you doing what you want to do right? . . . Have you located your passion as if this was your last night on earth?"

2

LIFE ON YOUR TERMS

This above all: to thine own self be true.

—*William Shakespeare,* Hamlet

Your thought patterns can be a wellspring of abundance to live life on your terms. But negative talk and self-doubt are a drain on your inner resources. Our relationships form the basis of our lives. Strong supportive relationships increase our happiness and contribute to holistic wealth. However, there are some relationships that can cause stress and negatively affect our mental well-being. The term *naysayers* is how I refer to the people and social forces who tap into negative thinking and undermine your belief in your own ability to create holistic wealth. Toxic naysayers are destructive to holistic wealth; they try to trap women into a narrative in which they're afraid of their goals, of embarrassment, of not being enough.

When your life situation changes and you're in a period of transition and vulnerability, whether by virtue of divorce, widowhood, job loss, or an illness or disability, the naysayers come crawling out of every crevice to tell you what to do. What follows are three types of toxic naysayers you will likely encounter at some point in life.

#1: THE CHRONIC NAYSAYERS

These are the naysayers who point out seeming "flaws" in your current situation, which they think should prevent you from achieving a goal or carrying out a particular task. They tell you that you shouldn't bother trying at all—because you don't have x, y, or z.

At the beginning of the summer, three months after my husband died, I was at home with my two babies, and I had my air-conditioning on. One naysayer, while over for a visit, peered at the thermostat on the wall as if examining a very rare and expensive piece of equipment and then told me I shouldn't turn on my air-conditioning because there was only one salary now, "and AC is expensive." Another naysayer told me I shouldn't even think of driving to Toronto from Ottawa (a five-hour drive) by myself, "because, you know, it's far and you're a woman driving alone." Another told me to "go hang out with your single friends now" because I was no longer married.

Chronic naysayers infiltrate every part of life and have no conversational boundaries, whether it's money, relationships, friendship—nothing is off limits. They try to force you into a box and make you believe you need to fit into it.

#2: THE LACK-OF-RESOURCES NAYSAYERS

These naysayers will mainly point to a lack of resources to stop you from going after your goals. One naysayer said to me, "Well, I guess you will never take another vacation, since there's only one salary now and you have two kids." After my husband died, I traveled all over the world—more than ever before. These naysayers had no idea that I had planned for the future and that my husband and I had put things in place to prevent financial fallout (see Part II of this book).

#3: THE "COMPARISON NELLY" NAYSAYERS

These naysayers will compare your current situation with that of your friends, family members, or just about anyone, really (including themselves and people from their childhood), and then tell you that you are somehow not like them (or don't have what they have), so you can't possibly achieve the way they are achieving. In my early days of widowhood, one of these comparison Nellys said to me, "You can't start a big project on your own, even though your friends have, because they have husbands to help them and, well, you don't." Concerning remarriage, another comparison Nelly said, "I met my husband in university, when we were young. Nobody is going to want you now with two children!"

Naysayers are everywhere, and they tend to embrace a scarcity mentality. They do not believe in the Law of Abundance, and they are oblivious to the fact that each of us is endowed with unique, God-given talents and a voice to carry out our true purpose in life. Naysayers are confidence-bashers and goal-destroyers who will toss you into a state of confusion, where you begin to second-guess your goals and lose valuable time to procrastination. This leads to feeling overwhelmed and paralyzed.

Widowhood at age thirty-one meant that no one in my age group within my social circle understood what I was going through. The pain and loneliness of grief was compounded by the fact that I was also an outlier. An anomaly. This was a different kind of loneliness. We all know what it means to feel like there's no one on our side. Perhaps you have encountered a similar situation of feeling powerless—after a divorce, job loss, domestic violence, or emotional abuse. Perhaps you were told you have the wrong accent, that you don't look "mainstream" enough, that you have the wrong skin color, that because you are an immigrant or a refugee you can't succeed. We all encounter these defining moments. Because naysayers employ a scarcity mentality, they will tell you that you lack resources and, as a result, you lack access to greater opportunity, success, and wealth.

When naysayers impose limiting beliefs, it affects the individual and collective power women have to achieve our dreams. Women whose families don't fit the traditional archetype, such as single moms and young widows, may be especially vulnerable. Many naysayers point to a supposed lack of financial resources, but this is a vast assumption to make, because a single-parent household need not lead to financial ruin. It is also a vast assumption to make that a woman's financial status will remain static over time or that a single mom has limited earning potential. Such a position freezes a life's opportunities in one moment in time. Imposing this narrative on young women has economic and societal repercussions writ large. According to the United Nations Population Fund 2018 State of the World Population report, nearly 40 percent of kids are being raised by single mothers in the United States. In 2016, there were 320 million children being raised by single-parent families across the globe.[6]

When people are given negative messages about women's prospects and they listen, it influences the economic outcomes of women and their families, which has an impact on poverty and the socioeconomic status of children. The result is that women may unconsciously hold themselves back professionally, get fewer salary increases and promotions over time, and become pigeonholed into stereotypical "female" roles (mother, caretaker, subordinate).

I want all women to know that they can achieve their dreams. You don't have to have a husband, boyfriend, or wealthy uncle. Many famous women went against the expectations of others to chart a new path forward, to set the direction of progress in their lives and for humanity: women such as Oprah Winfrey, Michelle Obama, Arianna Huffington, Shonda Rhimes, Harriet Tubman, Rosa Parks, Malala Yousafzai. Some of these women fought against the odds to achieve their goals while enduring life-threatening oppression.

In order for us to reorient how we view resources, we have to step away from the way resources are viewed by the naysayers and those with a scarcity mentality. Albert O. Hirschman, the influential development economist, articulated a difference between what he called "economic resources" and "moral resources." Hirschman's view is that when we think economically, we think that the more we deploy resources, the fewer there are left. He developed the idea of "moral resources" and argued that the more we deploy these types of resources, the more they grow. Moral resources are skills, relationships, collaboration, and knowledge. This is why this book is called

---

6. United Nations Population Fund (UNFPA), *State of the World Population 2018: The Power of Choice: Reproductive Rights and the Demographic Transition*, https://www.unfpa.org/sites/default/files/pub-pdf/UNFPA_PUB_2018_EN_SWP.pdf.

Holistic Wealth—achieving wealth holistically requires a preoccupation not just with financial resources but also with moral resources, plus a recognition that all of these resources are key in overcoming trauma and adversity and having a life well lived. Hirschman was a visionary, as these are the very resources needed when operating in uncertainty and disruption. Hirschman's iconic phrase, "proving Hamlet wrong," was about acting in the face of doubt and uncertainty and in the face of fear. This fear and doubt, Hirschman believed, is necessary for innovation and success. One of his famous essays was titled "The Principle of the Hiding Hand," which contained similar ideas to Adam Smith's "invisible hand" concept that was famously outlined in Smith's book *The Wealth of Nations*. Hirschman believed that when planning for the future, we should always anticipate unforeseen circumstances. We all need to prove the naysayers wrong and take back our power.

Dr. Martin Luther King Jr. defined power as "the ability to achieve purpose," adding that "whether [the power] is good or bad depends on the purpose."[7] Fundamental to holistic wealth is the understanding that each of us is endowed with the power we need to achieve purpose. Richard Emerson argues that power is not a thing but a relationship.[8] Power is therefore relational: your interests interact with the resources required to achieve them. If you can realize your interests entirely with your own resources, you have all the power you need. If acting on your interests requires access to someone else's resources to the same degree that acting on their interests requires access to yours, you can collaborate to create more power to achieve purpose.

---

7. Marshall Ganz, "People, Power and Change," lecture, John F. Kennedy School of Government, Harvard University, Cambridge, Massachusetts, 2018.
8. Richard M. Emerson, "Power-Dependence Relations," *American Sociological Review* 27, no. 1 (February 1962): 31–41.

In a lecture in my course at Harvard University, Professor Marshall Ganz, architect of the Obama presidential field campaign and author of *Why David Sometimes Wins: Leadership, Organization, and Strategy in the California Farm Worker Movement,* used the Montgomery bus boycott to illustrate how Rosa Parks's refusal to sit in one section of the bus sparked a movement where people with no financial resources or economic power worked to overthrow segregation laws, during a time of significant disruption. Your network is power and wealth, and tapping into the resources of your network can help you achieve your goals (see chapter 31). As my professor pointed out, "good strategizing is correcting the imbalance to move the fulcrum on which the balance rests to get more leverage out of the same resources. Good strategists learn to get more leverage from the resources that ARE available. Power is thus a matter of resources and resourcefulness." In other words, strategy is about turning "what you have" into "what you need" to get "what you want"—using the resources you have to achieve your goals, given constraints and opportunities.[9]

There will never be a "perfect time" to pursue your goals. You have now, and that's pretty much all you need. Surround yourself with positive influences. Let go of the naysayers who only serve to bog you down with negative messages, and find positive people who are excited about your future prospects. Some people were only meant to be a part of one aspect of your journey. If you can't take them with you into the next phase of your life, then that's okay; they have served their purpose. Don't look back, and don't overthink it.

Naysayers can't prevent your brilliance and purpose from entering the world. It will seep under doors like water flooding into a room. Its shafts will beam through windows like the

---

9. Marshall Ganz, "Strategy: Notes, Charts, and Questions," lecture, John F. Kennedy School of Government, Harvard University, Cambridge, Massachusetts, 2015.

dazzling rays on a bright, summery morning. Within the sunlight are galaxies and constellations filled with opportunities for you to take. Your radiance will materialize, even when you least expect it. All you have to do is create the environment for its manifestation and keep striving, keep going toward your mission.

Don't let naysayers sabotage your goals. Truly live your life on your terms.

Start planning and taking those baby steps toward your dreams now. Don't try to stick around to see if the naysayers will change. Your life can't depend on their timeline for change—it has to be yours. I know the guilt of feeling like you are walking away from your friendship, but think about it like this: You are stepping into your dreams. You are stepping into the life you want. You are stepping into your purpose, your eternity, and your future. So, say, "Hello, future, I am coming!"

3

A PERSONAL MISSION

> Your purpose in life is to find your purpose
> and give your whole heart and soul to it.
>
> *—Buddha*

Life has a way of eventually making us face our mortality head-on. It will make you stop and think about your impact on society. The legacy you leave lasts long after you are gone.

As I sat in the front row of the congregation at my husband's funeral, before some four hundred people who had turned out that day, and I listened to speaker after speaker utter similar words about Garfield, something became quite evident: whether he had died at fifty-four or even seventy-four or ninety-four instead of thirty-four, the script of his life would have been the same, because he knew his *values* and acted upon them in an intentional, proactive way—and by doing that, he touched many lives, and his legacy will live on even though he is gone. This was a true life lesson for me: we don't have to wait to create the life we want or to have impact on society. His wealth wasn't measured simply in monetary terms but in the many lives he had touched and, therefore, enriched.

If you were a spectator at your own funeral, what would you want your friends and family to remember you for most? What are the most prominent themes you would want to hear? What moments would you be most proud of?

Having a personal mission is a very powerful way to shape the answers to such questions. It is how you set the direction of progress and fundamental to an intentionally designed life. At a basic level, your personal mission has to be rooted in the story of you, the sum of your life experiences, and what you want to achieve in the future. It is like a blueprint for your life that is filled with action verbs and themes that you associate with achieving a sense of abundance, and which extends beyond material resources.

Our personal mission statement is a crystallization and the practical output that results from spiritual self-renewal in terms of setting the direction of progress in our life. It outlines our vision and our values. Viktor Frankl writes in *Man's Search for Meaning* that "we detect rather than invent our missions in life." This is where our intuition—our internal GPS system—comes into play. Each of us has an internal monitor or sense, a conscience, which gives us an awareness of our own uniqueness and the singular contributions that we can make. In Frankl's words, "Everyone has his own specific vocation or mission in life. Therein he cannot be replaced, nor can his life be repeated. Thus, everyone's task is as unique as is his specific opportunity to implement it." When we practice self-reflection and spiritual self-renewal (see chapter 19), setting the trajectory of progress in our lives comes naturally. We use our newly found self-awareness to examine our life's road maps and make certain that they accurately describe our goals in the form of a written personal mission statement that is unique to every person. As each of us can have different road maps along the way, constantly examining our mission and goals is necessary.

My uncle Aston Farquharson is the CEO of NuSpecies Corporation, based in New York City, a company that manufactures raw, organic natural health supplements. He was a corporate lawyer by training and on the path to becoming a vice president of a multinational company on Wall Street, but after his father (my grandfather) died of prostate cancer, my uncle reexamined his purpose and decided to take a different path in life. He made a vow to himself to try to make healthy supplements that would help the body heal and rebuild itself. He didn't just design a product—he designed a whole system around teaching people that the body, if given the right nutrition, can heal itself. He dedicated resources to counseling people on eating right and living a healthy lifestyle. His business was mission oriented from the get-go. It's now one of the most successful businesses in health supplements in New York City. He holds multiple patents and is currently expanding his business globally.

The mission statement of Kerry Wekelo, chief operating officer at Actualize Consulting, is "Making each day a great day." Kerry states, "This mission statement puts the way I live each day into one feeling. I came up with it while making a commitment to keep my day on a positive path. I use what I call my six principles: breathe, move, nourish, communicate, challenge, and routine. By incorporating these principles into my daily life, I increase my potential to make a great day."

Josh Hatcher, founder of Hatcher Media and Manlihood.com, a personal development website for men, has a personal mission statement. Hatcher's priorities—God, family, mentorship, and money (financial independence)—are evident in the way he lays out his personal mission statement. Notice how certain key phrases, such as service to God and humanity, mentorship, and building passive income streams, are used to outline his goals:

- (Why) Purpose: To live a life of love and service to God, my family, and my community.
- (What) Mission: To use my talents and abilities to enrich and lead in the lives of my family, my friends, my community, and all of those in my expanding circle of influence.
- (How) Vision: I will live as an ambassador of Christ and lead my family, while I find meaning and value in my work, while building passive income streams, and mentoring and encouraging men and women.
- Vision Simplified: Represent—Value—Build—Mentor—Encourage.

Kari Howe, who has spent her career at companies such as Zappos and Hulu and is now the director of learning and development at Drift, takes a somewhat different approach. In a written interview, she offered the following points for developing a mission statement.

- **How to go about writing a personal mission statement:** I'll go through lots of different exercises, mostly writing things down. I think: What values matter most to me? What words describe who I want to be in the year ahead? What do I want to accomplish in my personal and professional life? What do I want to be doing in six months that I'm not doing now? In twelve months? What inspires me? What are my superpowers?

- **Why have a personal mission statement?** It's sort of like your anchor for what you do—day in, day out, week in, week out. It's a place I can revisit to re-center myself and "get back on track" with what matters to me in my life. The process of writing one alone is enough to get really clear on what matters to you.
- **What do I do beyond creating a mission statement?** A mission statement alone will not help you achieve what you want. Taking on weekly or monthly exercises of setting personal goals can really help you achieve specific goals that all are anchored in or manifestations of your personal mission statement.
- **Kari's mission statement:** Through my strengths of drive, enthusiasm, and connection, I am a catalyst for people taking on creating their lives and having lives they love.

Holistic wealth happens by design; it results from a series of strategic decisions. It is not accidental or mired in mindless activities or driven by habits. Personal mission statements are an important component of an intentionally designed life, leadership, and personal development. It forces you to think deeply about your life, clarify its purpose, and identify what is truly important to you. A personal mission statement also forces you to clarify and express, as briefly as possible, your deepest values and aspirations. It imprints your values and purposes in your mind so they become a part of you. Take time to craft your own personal mission statement and integrate it into your weekly planning as a way to keep your vision constantly in front of you.

4

GOALS, WITH WISDOM

A calm and humble life will bring more happiness than the pursuit of success and the constant restlessness that comes with it.

—Albert Einstein

At twenty-nine, I was on an executive track, handpicked by my senior management to become a future leader in the organization. In less than two years, I would have become an executive through a fast-track program. But that was derailed when tragedy struck. I had to abandon those ambitions for a while. I had a baby who was eight weeks old at the time of my husband's passing, and I had to take extra time off work to deal with everything. I took exactly a year and a half off, during which I thought of the executive program sometimes and saw that various women who graduated had become executives, and I wondered what was happening to my life. Some of them had risen through the ranks and become senior executives. I was still just a young widow with two small children—seemingly on a fast track to nowhere.

Now I have come a full 180 degrees and realize that sometimes there are life lessons that have far greater significance than reaching the top at the age of thirty-one. We all have a unique road to follow, and that dictates our path. After my husband died, one of his friends called me out of the blue one day. She wanted to thank me for walking the path with him, and then she said to me, "But who better than you to walk with him? You brought him so much happiness and joy." The tears welled up in my eyes when I realized what she meant. I thought, "You mean this was a part of my life's purpose?" Yes, you bet! Part of my purpose in life was to be his wife, companion, and champion. His life on this earth was to be short, but it was punctuated by the joy and the love he had with his family.

Don't compare your journey with anyone else's. Not the job title or the salary or the perks. Here's the thing: it's now twelve years since my husband passed away, and at the time of writing this book, I have a deeply meaningful job where I am called to serve humanity. Still, I didn't go back into that executive training program. As a matter of fact, the program was scrapped. I was hand-picked again and put on another executive track years later, and I was led to my current job through the combination of life experience and knowledge I had accumulated.

In setting your goals, don't tie yourself to unrealistic expectations that everything will go as planned, so if you don't make partner of the law firm at thirty-five, you're not completely devastated. Also, be wise in your thoughts and confident in your unique path, so that if your colleague makes partner and you don't, you can celebrate with her and not feel like a failure. Your path *will* be different—it's supposed to be so. From a standpoint of holistic wealth, the obstructions to our goals hold considerable value, too.

BE A DETOUR CONQUEROR

For most of us, the path toward our goals is marked by short detours, some of them very rocky and winding. How do you handle yours? Do you obsess about the path you were once on? Or do you pat yourself on the back for conquering the detour? Consider that the path you were once on was meant to end when it did. Obsessing about plans lost or changed is a barrier to holistic wealth because it keeps you stuck in the past and unable to move forward.

Tell yourself this: *I am a conqueror. I am a detour slayer. And my goals and dreams don't exist in a vacuum. Every bit of my life is preparing me for something better, something greater!*

When you set your goals, do so knowing that there will be detours ahead. Know that some things will be out of your control. All things are on God's perfect timing. Put things in place and know that if a detour comes, you are a detour slayer. Achieving holistic wealth requires determination and grit. It requires an ability to pivot and change direction if need be. It requires that get-up-and-go attitude even in the face of tremendous obstacles.

MAKE GOALS ENJOYABLE

I can't count the number of times I've set goals to go to the gym or start a new healthy eating regimen and then blown them off. I've gone as far as paying the annual fee and then just didn't turn up. I drove past the gym, held my head straight, and pretended I didn't make the commitment. The truth is, I was never a gym person. So why did I keep setting these gym goals? I bought into the narrative that says the best way to lose weight is to join a gym. Only when I went on sabbatical and sought a new paradigm for my life did I start fulfilling my exercise goals.

If your goals don't excite you and whet your appetite, that's a problem. If you think about your goals and you'd rather play bingo at your grandmother's seniors club, that's another problem right there. Take the healthy recipes I developed, also started on my sabbatical, a sort of eating-for-self-renewal paradigm. If I had just set an objective to eat healthily, I would have blown this off, too. But I had begun employing a full systems-perspective to my entire life. A revolution of sorts. I developed these recipes because I love a certain type of healthy eating infused with herbs and spices and tropical ingredients. If I had based my healthy eating habits regimen on just bland salads, I wouldn't have stuck to my goals, because I'm not your average bland-salad-eating type. I'm a jazz-it-up type. I like spices and herbs and tropical fruits. Plus, I like grilling, and you can't grill salads, but I love grilled pineapple. I have a grilled pineapple recipe with butter rum sauce that includes spices like cinnamon, allspice, and nutmeg; a bit of darkened rum; and a little sugar for the butter rum sauce. That's pineapple completely jazzed up—and I'm excited already!

I have set goals without taking action sometimes because I didn't like the follow-up needed to execute them. If we constantly break promises to ourselves, we're training the brain to accept falling short on our goals as a habit. Once it becomes a habit, it's no problem if we do it over and over again. Goals need to be all jazzed up, not boring—and they're best firmly rooted in your personal mission.

Knowing yourself is critical to starting a revolution. Think of your goals as an arrow, not a cycle. We sometimes suffer burnout with our goals and the actions required to follow through because we're accustomed to doing things in a certain cyclical way. Stephen Jay Gould says that "time is sometimes a cycle and sometimes an arrow." Carrying out our goals with a cyclical viewpoint helps us to maintain our normal routines. Thinking of time as an arrow is more revolutionary in terms of the change we need—and in focusing our efforts. Think of your goals as an arrow with a precise target in order to create a revolution to start something new, to break out of the cycle.

Holistic wealth requires breaking out of the cycle—it requires focusing our efforts and being intentional with our desired goals. It requires a revolution to start something new and transform our current reality into something better. Holistic wealth requires setting goals that are like arrows with precise targets.

5

THE INCOMPARABLE YOU

There is something that you can do better than anyone else in the whole world. . . . Expressing your talents to fulfill needs creates unlimited wealth and abundance.

—*Deepak Chopra*

Comparison to others is the emperor of all emotional maladies. It kills the spirit and creates divisions in our social interactions. Each of us comprises 7 octillion atoms[10] and 37.2 trillion cells uniquely formed to manifest the beauty of something singular—our natural abilities and talents. When we try to walk in someone else's path and live their life instead of ours, we deny the universe a manifestation specially designed to drive humanity forward. How can we deny the universe the gift of our unique contributions that only we

10. Fiona MacDonald, "Mind-Blowing Facts About Your Body," ScienceAlert.com, November 6, 2016, https://www.sciencealert.com.

ourselves can manifest in this world? Comparison to others also puts you into a lack-and-scarcity frame of mind, and when we compare ourselves to others based on money, it's one of the most toxic financial blocks.

The fundamental reason why sometimes we don't manifest our unique contributions or truly live out our purpose is that we don't really believe we can do it. We stand naked and vulnerable, and we look around at others, and we say, "Can I really do this?" That vulnerability causes doubt and fear, and when we compare our nascent selves with someone who is more advanced in whatever endeavor we are thinking of pursuing, we shrink into a thought like "This won't ever happen for me." Comparing ourselves to others is one of the most toxic things we can do.

Meiyoko Taylor, a two-time bestselling author and celebrity personal development coach, concurs. In an interview, he said he believes comparison is the "suppressor of all gifts and the destroyer of our life's true aspirations. When you begin to compare yourself to others, you start to focus on everything around you instead of what's most important. Your life becomes centered around what other people think, do, and what their expectations are of you. As a result, you begin to exist in a world where your passions begin to die within you."

Meiyoko recounted the lowest point in his life:

> I remember when I had hit rock bottom in my life. Because I measured success by everyone and everything else but my own thoughts, I found myself completely miserable. I was working at a job that I hated but everyone told me I should be happy because it was a great profession. My entire design for my life was operating based on the comparison of others. It wasn't before long that I became severely

> overweight, my health was failing, and I didn't know who I was anymore. I learned that this constant behavior of comparing myself to people caused me to lose my identity. This is why it is so dangerous to build your lifestyle this way.

If you outline a personal mission for yourself and focus on only your mission, you become empowered to avoid comparisons. You become a soldier for your mission—you have no time to think about what anyone else is doing or achieving, because you are marching toward your goals. Once you set the direction of progress in your life, you create history.

This is a historic moment. Why? you may ask. Because there will only ever be one you, in one moment of time where you have set the wheels in motion to start living out your purpose in life. So, march forward into history and claim your spot. Do as Michelle Obama did with her historic moment as the first African American First Lady, and shine in your moment. There is room for all of us in this wide, big universe, and we can all have our own slice of the pie because we are all different and have an individual path in life that is tied to our specific talents and purpose. This is the Law of Abundance at work!

Use spiritual self-renewal to reconnect to who you are and what you really want in life. If you're not happy in life, be brutally honest with yourself about why that is. Regardless of what others think your life looks like from the outside, embrace what's true for you.

In doing this, examine what you are gifted with, your specific skills and talents. Having figured this out, you may start to pursue a path that can add value to other people's paths. When you are aligned with your passion and purpose, you never have to compare yourself with anyone else again. Understand that you have your own individual journey, and you are equipped with all you need to establish your own legacy.

DEFINE SUCCESS ON YOUR TERMS

Determine what success means to you. It may be far more than just riches and financial wealth, more than keeping up with the Joneses.

It seems in our early twenties we all start life at the same starting line. We graduate from university and enter the work world as young professionals eager to prove we have what it takes to succeed. By the time our early thirties (and for some, our late twenties) roll around, we start to suffer various setbacks. Some people experience transformational setbacks, such as the death of a spouse or a child or even a life-altering divorce. Others of us seem to be spared the more traumatic experiences but suffer the typical career or everyday type of setbacks.

It is easy to sink into self-pity when we're faced with losses and setbacks, but everyone has challenges. In my case, I was the only one in my peer group who was suddenly widowed at the age of thirty-one, with two young kids.

If you are in a similar situation where you are the only one in your peer group who hasn't achieved a certain milestone or who has suffered a life-altering setback, know that everything in life is temporary. If you have also encountered some naysayers in your life, know that your true friends will not forsake you because of personal circumstances. Tragedy and setbacks have a way of revealing our true friends. If your friends seem uncomfortable with you because you're suddenly single after a break-up, a divorce, or the death of a spouse, rest assured that they probably weren't true friends, anyway.

LET GO OF MOM GUILT

Soon after my husband passed away, I realized it would be almost impossible to keep up with the other moms who had their kids in a million extracurricular activities, were presidents of the school PTA, and always brought homemade cookies to school and work. I had to make peace with the notion that I wouldn't be able to compete or keep score. After all, I had just given birth and was dealing with the death of my husband. I was still in that phase where my eight-week-old, Alex, was waking up for feedings every two hours like clockwork, and I was physically exhausted from the loss of sleep and the soul-sucking grief.

And yet, I worried about things like my oldest child not being enrolled in swimming lessons or gymnastics for maybe a year, at least not until I had the chance to get my head around transitioning through this tragedy. In some ways, I still think about how I could have done better.

This kind of mom guilt keeps us trapped in a cycle of feeling like we're never doing enough. Even years later, when my boys were enrolled in competitive soccer and going to matches and training six times a week, it still didn't feel like enough. In addition, I felt like I had to always be there to support them. Our weekends were hijacked by soccer tournaments and training. I walked into work on a Monday morning feeling like a zombie. What's more, I felt that since my husband died and the boys lost their father, I had to compensate for their loss by doing everything I possibly could, and more—I needed to be superhuman to manage the demands, which was exceedingly stressful. Then after COVID-19 hit and I worked from home while homeschooling three kids, the mom guilt started again. A typical day homeschooling during the first phase of lockdown started with sorting through about forty emails from ten to fourteen different teachers, spanning three different grade levels and three different schools. For moms, letting go of mom guilt is key to recovering from disruption.

Every woman has her own story, her own set of obstacles, and you shouldn't compare your obstacles with mine or anyone else's. A better way is to be patient with ourselves and realize that it will work out in the end. Don't feel that you have to overcompensate. Rather, focus on what you do and have done. Pay attention to the tiny steps you've made. You've come a long way, baby! Cheer yourself on and keep telling yourself that you're killing this mom thing!

THE TRIPLE HELIX FOR WOMEN

Women are dealing with a triple helix of responsibilities—career, home, and kids. This is a dangerous proposition for women, and I'll tell you why. Women have also been sold the lie that we can have it all: we can kill it in our careers, be Martha Stewart at home, and have perfect children. So, we follow the patriarchal system and buy into this notion of striving for perfection in all areas, and then we get disappointed when it sometimes doesn't work out. Men are okay with killing it in just one area, with not being superdads—their fathers weren't superdads; their grandfathers weren't superdads. But check how many women had supermoms. I would say more women would say they had supermoms than superdads. We think of our mothers, and we want to set the example in our homes that they set in theirs.

When the fallout and disruption from trauma, death, divorce, or job loss enters our lives and we have pinned our identities as women on this lie that we can have it all at the same time and do it all perfectly and seamlessly, what happens when we can't live up to what we have socially constructed as our ideal? Do we feel shame and embarrassment because we had to take a step back from our careers to deal with the fallout? I can tell you now that women bear the brunt in these situations. For women of color it's even more challenging. Women of color head more single-family households, in which they are the main breadwinners, yet they earn less and have lower job prospects. In the US, almost 39 percent of Black families headed by women live in poverty; the rate of poverty is almost 41 percent in Hispanic families headed by women and almost 30 percent in Asian American families headed by women. "Among all other ethnic groups, Native American female-headed families with children had the highest poverty rate. More than two in five (42.6 percent) live in poverty."[11] In an article for the *New York Observer* (now known as the *Observer*), I spoke about this "emaciation effect," a phenomenon that affects people of color who have to deal with regular stressors in addition to a lifetime of racial discrimination, which also affects our ability to achieve holistic wealth.

BLACK AND MINORITY WOMEN DURING COVID-19

Due to the effects of COVID-19, there's a revolution happening—it's been called both "the great awakening" and "the great resignation wave." As economies began reopening, the world saw a record number of people quitting their jobs. In April 2021, that exodus amounted to four million US workers, or 2.7 percent of the US workforce.[12] What's even more startling are the numbers for Black professionals leaving their

---

11. "Single Mother Statistics," Single Mother Guide, updated June 14, 2019, https://singlemotherguide.com/single-mother-statistics/.
12. Lauren Weber, "Forget Going Back to the Office—People Are Just Quitting Instead," *Wall Street Journal*, June 13, 2021, https://www.wsj.com/articles/forget-going-back-to-the-officepeople-are-just-quitting-instead-11623576602.

place of work. A recent survey from Future Forum highlighted that only 3 percent of Black knowledge workers surveyed want to go back to the office full-time.[13]

For many of us, these results are not surprising. Black women often suffer microaggressions and discrimination at work, and most feel like they don't belong in their workplaces. Many feel like they have to "code-switch"—adjust the way they talk, look, or behave just to fit in. Bit by bit, it feels like death by a thousand cuts—and there have been reports of suicidal thoughts due to racial discrimination at work.

For many Black women, their work has been undervalued and underrecognized for far too long. As Celina Caesar-Chavannes, author of *Can You Hear Me Know?: How I Found My Voice and Learned to Live with Passion and Purpose*, stated in an interview on episode 12 of the *Holistic Wealth* podcast, "Even when we are given a seat at the table, we're not on the menu." Remote work helped Black women navigate those issues, and created a safe space to process their feelings during the unprecedented and historic protests that ensued in the summer of 2020 following the death of George Floyd at the hands of the police, which commentators have compared to the uprisings in 125 cities in the aftermath of the assassination of Martin Luther King Jr. in 1968.

Leslie Forde, whom I recently interviewed on the *Holistic Wealth* podcast, is also the founder of Allies @ Work, an initiative aimed at helping workplaces design diversity programs. She conducted a pandemic survey of 2,000 parents (97 percent moms), which revealed that the return to work is an emotionally charged, incredibly complicated issue that most mothers are trying to navigate. Many women simply don't want to go

13. Sheela Subramanian, "A New Era of Workplace Inclusion: Moving from Retrofit to Redesign," Future Forum, March 11, 2021, https://futureforum.com/2021/03/11/dismantling-the-office-moving-from-retrofit-to-redesign/.

back to work—at least not in the way that they worked before. Leslie notes that "performative displays of busyness" and a "culture of captive time" have kept workers in their cubicles from nine to five, which is exacerbated by workplaces lacking sufficient supports for Black professionals.

Black women have shouldered the burden of an entire community ravaged by the effects of COVID-19. Studies show that biologically, Black women are on average 7.5 years older than white women because of the effects of racism. At the Institute on Holistic Wealth, we've incorporated a module on anti-racism in the Certified Holistic Wealth™ Consultant Program to help empower women, and especially women of color. The Holistic Wealth Generation is demanding that their voices be heard.

As employers look to design the workplaces of the future, listening to employees and moving the needle on the employee experience as it relates to anti-racism and diversity will be critical. In our organizations and teams—and as a society in general—we can't collectively master the art of recovery from disruption until there's social justice for all, which is a critical part of holistic wealth.

To drive all of humanity forward, we all need to embrace the holistic wealth mindset. Feminism needs to work for all women—not just some women. On episode 41 of the *Holistic Wealth* podcast I interviewed Eve Rodsky, *New York Times* bestselling author of *Fair Play: A Game-Changing Solution for When You Have Too Much to Do* and *Find Your Unicorn Space: Reclaim Your Creative Life in a Too-Busy World.* Eve shared her thoughts on white feminism: "It's incumbent on white-presenting women that we understand what 'care feminism' is, that we are not this boss feminism, this individualistic feminism—that notion has to be burned, and we have to come back to the table to recognize everybody's lived experience, and to fight for other people's lived experiences."

DECIDE ON YOUR UNIQUE PATH

Everyone has a path in life. We suffer losses at different stages—some of us suffer transformational setbacks earlier than others. Our situation can serve as a reminder that we're unique and meant to leave our own mark on the world.

A vital part of overcoming the feeling of being behind is knowing you're on a path toward achieving holistic wealth—and embracing it. Holistic wealth is also about embracing how your life is unfolding in ways that can help you specialize in a field, follow something you're interested in, pursue new experiences, or perhaps transition into a new career.

At each stage of our lives, we make sacrifices—calculated decisions that allow us to prioritize certain aspects, knowingly putting some life goals on the back burner to get something more pressing done now.

Part of self-assessment and spiritual self-renewal means really acknowledging that such decisions are conscious. Perspective is everything. If, for example, you put your career on hold to take care of family, like I did after my husband died, know that nurturing young kids or taking care of elderly parents is an opportunity. The validity of some decisions cannot be assessed based on monetary gain or the promise of fame or fortune.

These sacrifices may cause perceived "setbacks" because they're not considered part of society's milestones or indicators of success or wealth. However, we know the relative value of these activities to the health and well-being of our families, and often they are priceless.

Have you suffered a perceived setback? Do a thorough self-assessment, and you might just find that you probably didn't really suffer a setback at all. The incomparable you also includes embracing the circumstances that demand sacrifices on your part to add to the well-being and overall health of your families and loved ones.

6

A SABBATICAL

And this our life, exempt from public haunt,
Finds tongues in trees, books in the running
brooks,
Sermons in stones, and good in everything.

—*William Shakespeare,* As You Like It

After my husband died, I realized I needed to take a break to do some soul-searching. I took a one-year unpaid sabbatical—I packed up my kids and my things, put our stuff in a forty-foot storage container, and headed to beautiful, sunny Jamaica.

I knew my search for answers amidst the unexplainable would only be possible through drastic action. I had the urge to make peace with something completely out of my hands. Something that I hadn't had a chance to fight for. Something that required a whole year to find the cause. Something for which the doctors would have to surrender in defeat. This theme of making peace with things that are not in our control recurs in the work of Mughal-era statesman and poet Abdur Rahim Khanan, also known as "master of the couplet." The *art of the couplet* is to condense worlds of wisdom and meaning into a tiny vessel—or for the poet, only a couple of lines or stanzas. In his most celebrated work, the *Dohavali* (an "array of couplets"), he writes, "The way of truth means giving up the world."

I didn't realize what I was doing when I decided to take a sabbatical. To find my truth, I gave up the world and packed what was left of my belongings into that forty-foot container. I sold most of my furniture, sold my car, sold his car. I sold most things I had in my garage, including tools and equipment. I also rented our home to a lovely young couple. I felt like I needed to seek answers to the mysteries surrounding my husband's death in order to move forward.

Once my sabbatical started, I experienced a different kind of healing. As Shakespeare suggests in the epigraph of this chapter, I left a life "exempt from public haunt." I found "tongues in trees, books in the running brooks, / [and] sermons in stones." I came alive in examining brooks. The water ever changing, ever moving, beating on tiny rocks swooshing to and fro; its very movement was effortless, simple, and effervescent. Just the notion of looking at a brook with fresh eyes, with a new curiosity, made me feel new connections; my brain became engrossed and took millions of tiny frames from different angles, and started making new neural pathways.

I took solace in the mountains where I could reinvent myself amidst jagged ocean cliffs. The house where I stayed was nestled on a hill, perched eight hundred feet above sea level, in Belvedere Heights, where mountains soared. Like the nest of a Jamaican hummingbird, the house is set intricately into the landscape. It became my mountain retreat, overlooking the city and tucked into nature, so that I woke up to stunning magnificence every morning. The hill at the rear of the house was an orchard—cherries and apples seemed to sing a chorus in concert with the gentle breeze.

In Jamaica, it seems leisure time always abounds. The island is naturally blessed with a large food surplus. In the old days, its inhabitants were fishermen, farmers, and hunters. However, this was not what the early missionaries arriving on the island in the early 1800s had in mind for the islanders as a way of life. Nevertheless, its history and culture, deeply rooted in its past, are what gives the country its unique flavor. From the gospel according to Bob Marley to the food—the jerk stalls that pepper the countryside and fill the air with flavors for miles—everything combines to create an environment of tropical laid-back vibes.

One of my favorite places on sabbatical was Port Royal. I often visited the Morgan's Harbour Hotel for lunch or dinner. This was the same hotel and yacht club used in the James Bond movie *Dr. No.* The complex has an open-air restaurant and bar area, and I would often eat on the same wooden dock shown in the *Dr. No* movie. The dock sits directly atop spectacular emerald water—it was as if you were having a gourmet meal on a raft, with waves competing to touch your toes. Some of the most succulent seafood dishes, plus a world-famous piña colada, were served atop that floating restaurant raft. My other favorite place? The Blue Lagoon in Portland, Jamaica, that looked like an oversize *Alice in Wonderland* teacup, with the deepest turquoise waters you've ever seen, surrounded by rain forests around its circumference. You would think you were Alice and you'd found the center of the universe, and that this secret fantasyland was reserved just for fellow Alices!

Many great writers have written about life-changing sabbaticals. Elizabeth Gilbert in *Eat Pray Love* did not explicitly refer to her time traveling as a sabbatical, but, in essence, it can be described as such, given that she was free to do as she wanted (even though she was writing her memoir). Her divorce was also a catalyst for seeking answers and a higher purpose. Similarly, Cheryl Strayed in *Wild* took on a hiking journey on the Pacific Crest Trail after her mother died.

On my sabbatical I stood at an inflection point, with my past behind me and my future before me, and I encountered a revelation: I could choose to live a life of service to others rather than one of selfish pursuits. The Motivation from Within framework came from this time when I could shut out all the noise, tune in to my intuition, and rediscover my purpose in life.

I recall one day while on sabbatical, my son Matthew had weekend homework. It was simply to go to the beach and pick up seashells, observe the different textures and colors, collect as many varieties as possible, and bring them to school on Monday morning. That homework assignment was an epiphany for me. This is how children learn in different cultures and contexts. To walk on the beach, pick up seashells, and simply experience them in their glory was like heaven. And that assignment still teaches me to this day. That sabbatical taught us to really live in the moment—to be able to observe nature around us and revel in it. This is the Law of Natural Harmony and Balance at its finest: living mindfully within the present moment. While walking on the sand on the beach, I could see the seashells, whole and cracked ones littered against the white sand around my feet. Some of the shells were colored with tropical apricot and turquoise hues, like someone gently brushed a stroke of color, from the finest paintbrush, on their bright white, pearly canvas. As I looked further down the beach, I saw the foam from the waves as it met with rock formations—rocks that simply sat there, waiting for the sea to envelop them with its thick, white, foamy essence. The rocks stood firm and patient, waiting for the waves to lavish them with unbridled attention—to make a splash, withdraw, and then envelop them with thick, lusty white foam again.

I walk out closer to some smaller rocks, and I see crabs and rocks in a nature dance. The rocks have rolled out their green mossy carpet for the small crabs to climb atop them to perch and rest. The crabs are happy as they lie on their soft carpet and huddle in threes and fours, like gossipy schoolgirls talking about their latest crush. I feel a surge of happiness just looking at them, just realizing that I am observing nature in a way I have never done before.

For my two boys, it was the same. During that time, we spent many weekends on the beach. It taught us multiple lessons; the waves, receding and pulling back again in a never-ending cycle, spoke to me about life, rebirth, and new beginnings. It is said that the sound of waves crashing and then receding can help to activate the parasympathetic nervous system, slowing us down and promoting relaxation.

There are many ways to take a sabbatical and make it beneficial both professionally and emotionally. (Go to www.instituteonholisticwealth.com to take the online course on how to prepare for a sabbatical.) Taking a sabbatical was a healing journey, and I learned many life lessons. I even learned how to travel on less than ten dollars a day in premium-priced, tropical Jamaica. My framework for taking a sabbatical abroad can also be re-created at home. After COVID-19, some people might not be comfortable traveling, or there may be travel restrictions, so a two-to-three-week wellness sabbatical at home is something to explore, and can be part of a recovery and renewal process, too. If you feel like you need additional help with healing from trauma or upheaval, the Institute on Holistic Wealth also has a course called Holistic Healing that can be combined with the sabbatical course. During COVID-19, my extended family embarked on a charity program to help a small rural community in Jamaica struggling through the pandemic. After I started the *Holistic Wealth* podcast, I reached out to international donors, and now my family and I (in partnership with the Institute on Holistic Wealth) are collaborating on a multimillion-dollar project to roll out alternative holistic learning centers for youth all across Jamaica—teaching skills to enable youth to become economically empowered and resilient.

Taking a sabbatical can be just as exciting as it is intimidating. A sabbatical can mean unimaginable self-discovery as you take time off to study or explore options, travel, learn new skills, and see the world. A sabbatical can ignite your passions and help you find your true purpose in life, as it allows you the free time to explore creative endeavors and helps you to sort through short- and medium-term goals. It allows you to think about big-picture goals, and to solidify your dreams and desires, and to put in place a plan of action. A sabbatical helps you to design an intentional life going forward. It allows you to discover your unique talents and to seek your higher self through spiritual self-renewal. On sabbatical, you can become your most authentic self. Once your passions are ignited, it becomes easier to find success in whatever field you choose. This time, given by you to yourself, is an invaluable resource for your well-being.

7

LIFE WITHIN EACH MOMENT

Count each day as a separate life.

—Lucius Annaeus Seneca

Time is a precious resource, more precious than silver and gold. If we were to "count each day as a separate life," as Lucius Seneca thought, we might truly live within each moment. After my husband died, I had a habit of compulsively reconstructing the events of the night in question—something that consumed and haunted me. It was as if I were on my own planet. Not really present here with everyone else, but in my own world reconstructing the scenes in Technicolor: the nurses shuttling around in the emergency room, dispensing medication, checking charts; the sharp smell of formaldehyde in the air. For almost a year afterward, I smelled formaldehyde everywhere. I had firmly situated myself in the past, not being mindful of the present. How do you learn to resituate yourself in a world where your soul mate no longer exists?

When I wasn't reconstructing events in the emergency room, I was thinking about where he might be. Was he in heaven singing with the angels happily without me? I was effectively straddling two worlds: the past, and some unknown form that wasn't really the future but a celestial version of a place we might all end up in. As C. S. Lewis wrote in *A Grief Observed,* "There is sort of an invisible blanket between the world and me." Was my husband really up there, enjoying his time singing with the angels, while I was here, left to struggle with our two babies? "You have got to be kidding me," I thought. Maybe he was there in some celestial-looking workshop, gently carving and preening his wings. At some point, I realized I had to start living in the present and cease thinking about this fantasia land and what Garfield might be doing there. These fantasies only served to amplify my feelings of helplessness, with no practical or therapeutic benefits.

As human beings we waste too many precious moments. On wasted moments and living in the present, Seneca once wrote the following:

> It is not that we have a short space of time, but that we waste much of it. Life is long enough, and it has been given in sufficiently generous measure to allow the accomplishment of the very greatest things if the whole of it is well invested. But when it is squandered in luxury and carelessness, when it is devoted to no good end, forced at last by the ultimate necessity, we

> perceive that it has passed away before we were aware that it was passing.[14]

Without spiritual self-renewal, it is extremely difficult to live within each moment. Without spiritual self-renewal, we live with the ghosts of the past and carry them with us to the future, effectively robbing ourselves of the present and never fulfilling our destiny and purpose.

Rediscovering my intuition on my sabbatical truly taught me how to live in each moment, to be completely present and one hundred percent intentional about it. There was no multitasking or thinking about the next chore, nothing but having my mind wrapped around one thing in the present.

It is easy to be carried away with ruminating about the past and worrying about the future. We waste precious seconds, minutes, hours doing this every single day. When we stop judging our experiences, we become less reactive and better able to tolerate difficulty. We become more resilient—and better able to recover from disruption. Have you ever felt like your mind is a slideshow and it just jumps from one frame to the next? There is no calm or stillness present. We leap from one thought to the next, often with frantic worry—sometimes about the mundane, like what to have for dinner, or whether the kids need shoes. The list goes on and on.

Figure 1 below presents a diagram that shows how a state of mindlessness in various aspects of our lives is counter to achieving holistic wealth and can lead to stunted potential.

---

14. Lucius Annaeus Seneca, "On the Shortness of Life," trans. John W. Basore, Loeb Classical Library (London: William Heinemann, 1932), http://www.forumromanum.org/literature/seneca_younger/brev_e.html.

Figure 1: A State of Mindlessness Is Counter to Achieving Holistic Wealth

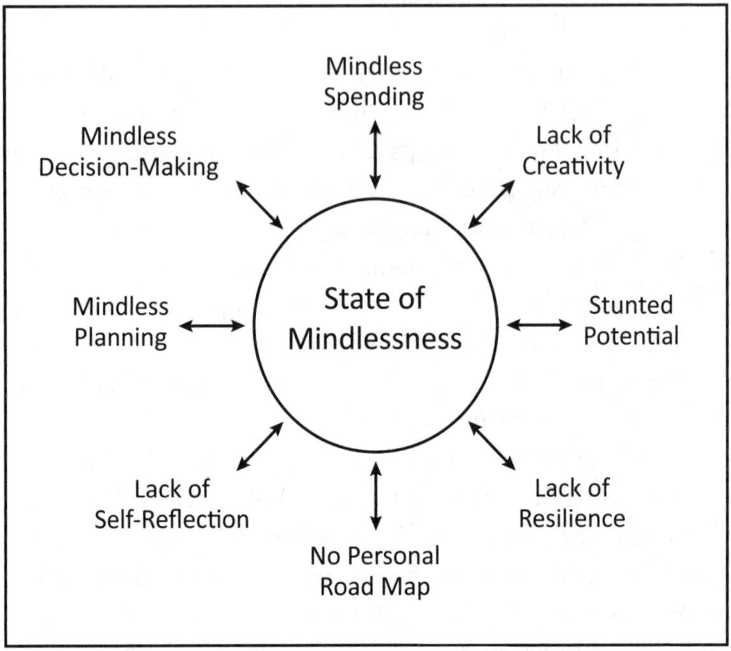

Mindless Spending

Mindless Decision-Making

Lack of Creativity

Mindless Planning

State of Mindlessness

Stunted Potential

Lack of Self-Reflection

Lack of Resilience

No Personal Road Map

From the Institute on Holistic Wealth

When we get bogged down with the busyness of life, there is no time to truly live within each moment. There is no time for self-reflection, spiritual self-renewal, or even to notice the fleeting moments that pass us by. We can't seek the truth about ourselves to chart a way forward. The time we spend *truly living* is thus minuscule. We are constantly wishing our lives away. When we are at our desks at work, we wish we were on vacation. We appoint a time for retirement when we shall "truly live," and then we wait for that time to come. At that point, we will truly enjoy life! We don't know whether this time will even be granted to us, but we proudly plan on it as if we know the exact date we will die.

In an interview, Wade Brill, cofounder of Centered in the City, a coaching collective rooted in mindfulness, self-development, and connection, noted that "we waste moments when we are not present. If our minds race to the future, we tend to be consumed with thoughts associated with planning, strategizing, negotiating, or striving. And if we let our minds get stuck in the past, we are typically trapped in story lines of self-doubt or wishing scenarios would have played out differently. When our mind is either in the past or future, we are missing the richness of life in this present moment. And we can never get that moment back."

Living in the moment means connecting to our senses and letting our mind focus on feeling alive. For instance, in any given moment, we can connect to our breath, noticing the length and temperature of it. We can taste each bite of food. We can listen deeply to sounds around us or fully immerse ourselves in the conversation we are having. We can pause to look at our surroundings and notice the signs on buildings, the color of moss on trees, or the lines on people's faces. Being present helps us slow down the experience of time and fully enjoy the gifts that are available now. Life, within each moment, contains an entire universe of riches.

8

THE NATURAL WORLD AROUND YOU

> Nature works with broad pastels when she
>   paints.
> Yet on this day I feel the recompense
> Of skies and colours that flourish beyond
>   constraints.
> For me you are the sum of all these things,
> Clouds, trees, hills, dales and flitting wings.
>
> —*William Shakespeare, "Sonnet VI"*

Mountains that tower like Olympian gods and rivers that flow to their own natural rhythm and beat punctuate the landscapes of some of the most beautiful places in the world. I'm not sure how we can fully appreciate life without seeing the natural glory that abounds, and, I kid you not, the mountains that swell from the road and seem to touch the sky in Jamaica, though awe-inspiring, are not the same as the ones in the Ka'a'awa Valley in Kualoa Ranch,

Hawai'i. The Swiss Alps and the North Shore mountains in Vancouver, British Columbia, are different in their rugged, forested slopes—not to mention the snowcapped mountains in Iran and the Himalayas in Asia—none of them are the same. I have seen them all, and they pay homage to a world where nature is meant to awe and inspire.

Seven months before my husband died, we went on a trip. This ended up being our first and last major trip to Europe. We visited Paris, Stuttgart, Brussels, and Geneva. I was about twelve weeks pregnant with Alex, and this was to be our last hurrah before becoming parents of two boys. The only things he bought on that trip were a pair of Pumas and a green golf shirt in Geneva, which he ended up wearing to the hospital on the night of his death. I recall pleading with him in Geneva just to buy one thing as a reminder for him of our trip, and so he picked up those two items in a store. The golf shirt and shoes were among the things in the white plastic bag given to me at the hospital.

Grief created a psychic cavity that nothing could fill. My grief stood like a medieval city with no walls, no fortress, no army—alone and vulnerable. It was traveling and spending copious amounts of time in nature that allowed me to see that all of creation was rooting for me. My husband died at the dawn of spring in April, and, in the days that followed, I felt almost betrayed by Mother Nature. She didn't seem to acknowledge my pain and grief. Her blossoms bloomed, and she seemed to come alive when my very soul felt crushed under the weight of an avalanche of intense pain. I was frozen in the cold death grip of winter in my heart, even though outside it was spring.

My husband loved nature, and he planted flowers and created a living garden, with pink and white peonies and other beautiful flowers, at the front of our house in Ottawa. Those flowers began to bloom in the weeks after he died. I felt like my heart was going to burst. They were coming to life, and he was gone.

On my sabbatical, while hiking in the world-famous Blue Mountains—home to more than eight hundred species of endemic plants and more than two hundred species of resident and migrant birds—I experienced the sights and sounds of nature. Birds woke me up in the morning and sang me to sleep at night. It is said that the patron saint of animals, Saint Francis of Assisi, had a special relationship with birds. Birds often symbolize spiritual freedom and growth. Saint Francis of Assisi is famous for preaching the sermon of the birds, found in *The Little Flowers of St. Francis, Actus B. Francisci et Sociorum Ejus*, Ugolino Brunforte:

> In every beat of your wings and every note of your songs, praise him. He has given you the greatest of gifts, the freedom of the air. You neither sow, nor reap, yet God provides for you the most delicious food, rivers, and lakes to quench your thirst, mountains, and valleys for your home, tall trees to build your nests, and the most beautiful clothing: a change of feathers with every season.

I realized that, in fact, nature hadn't betrayed me, but she was put there to ensure my very survival—and she was rooting for me. I just needed to see her and to experience her in a way I had never done before. I needed to spend time with her, in her bosom and womb, to soak up her healing powers and beauty.

As I started doing that, I realized the symbiotic relationship we have with nature. She was a part of me, and I was a part of her. My husband, though he was gone, was also a part of this larger creation. As Shakespeare's line at this chapter's opening states, I indeed felt nature's recompense, and all the beauty was there to help me really live and flourish. Like flowers that grow and thrive, and then die, rot, and go back to the earth that gave birth to them, so, too, do we flourish and grow and then die; we become the sum of all these things: clouds, trees, hills, dales, and flitting wings.

Scientific studies prove that the more time spent in awe-inspiring natural settings, the better our well-being. Nature is perhaps the most prominent elicitor of awe because of its sheer vastness and beauty. I reached out to Summer Allen, PhD, Research Fellow at the Greater Good Science Center at the University of California, Berkeley, which reports on groundbreaking research into the roots of compassion, happiness, and altruism. In September 2018, Summer wrote a white paper titled *The Science of Awe*, which opens with these words:

> If you've hiked among giant sequoias, stood in front of the Taj Mahal, or observed a particularly virtuosic musical performance, you may have experienced the mysterious and complex emotion known as "awe."
>
> Awe experiences are self-transcendent. They shift our attention away from ourselves, make us feel like we are part of something greater than ourselves, and make us more generous toward others.

Summer then sent me another article with additional scientific evidence titled "Awe in Nature Heals: Evidence from Military Veterans, At-Risk Youth, and College Students," published in June 2018.[15] The paper consisted of a study of 124 military veterans and youth from underserved communities

15. Craig L. Anderson, Maria Monroy, and Dacher Keltner, "Awe in Nature Heals: Evidence from Military Veterans, At-Risk Youth, and College Students," *Emotion* 18, no. 8 (December 2018).

(38 percent female) who participated in either one-day or four-day white water rafting trips organized by the Sierra Club Outdoors organization. The study concluded that "the awe experienced by military veterans and youth from underserved communities while white water rafting, above and beyond all the other positive emotions measured, predicted changes in well-being and stress-related symptoms one week later."

I believe that nature, and our environment, is part of our inherited natural wealth. I believe that vast oceans, forests, and mountains were put here to ensure our very survival and growth. By spending time in nature, we access holistic wealth through its physical, spiritual, and emotional benefits. Our environment helps us to succeed and build successful lives. We have a symbiotic relationship with nature whereby human beings are also an asset to nature, in that we are here to help protect and care for our environment, as well as benefit from it. We have a responsibility to address the grand environmental challenges of our time.

Part of our holistic wealth can be destroyed by events like climate change and ocean pollution. Environmental disasters like forest fires, flooding, and hurricanes can threaten our lives, destroy communities, and wipe out physical assets. A recently released report from the United Nations on biodiversity states that "nature is in more trouble now than at any other time in human history, with extinction looming over 1 million species of plants and animals."[16] Preserving our biodiversity and natural habitat is critical to stemming the tide of climate change. At the outset of the COVID-19 pandemic, many experts

---

16. United Nations report from the Intergovernmental Science-Policy Platform on Biodiversity and Ecosystem Services (IPBES), summary approved at the seventh session of the IPBES plenary meeting on April 29–May 4, 2019, in Paris, France, https://www.un.org/sustainabledevelopment/blog/2019/05/nature-decline-unprecedented-report/.

suggested that humanity's destruction of biodiversity had created the conditions for new viruses such as COVID-19 to emerge—which has caused catastrophic health and economic impacts across the globe. A new discipline called "planetary health" is emerging that focuses on the strong connections between the well-being of humans and entire ecosystems.

The Bank of Canada has now officially recognized the effects of climate change on the economy, and for the first time it will incorporate climate change as a "top weak spot" in its assessments of financial stability. Climate change is a threat to infrastructure, and even pension funds—it might even affect our ability to retire well. Nature is therefore an important part of how we access holistic wealth. Nature is an asset in our holistic wealth bank account. When we don't address environmental challenges, we make withdrawals from our holistic wealth bank account that have generational consequences. We rob future generations of being able to fully achieve holistic wealth.

9

ROAD TRIPS

> Once a year, go on a road trip.
>
> —*The Dalai Lama*

Road trips can be life altering. You learn about yourself: how you can improvise, how you react in different situations, how you appreciate beauty, how you adjust to changing altitude, how you relate to people when you're not stressed, and much more. Road trips allow us the time to think and reflect, to shift into a state of mindfulness. For these reasons and more, road trips are an asset of holistic wealth; like most travel, they enrich our lives with experiences, new vistas, and a sense of expanded time to contemplate the direction we're heading in.

Many business ideas and life-changing moments happen on the long stretches of road ahead of us as we pass by natural greenery, forests, oceans, and deserts. The open road allows the mind to ponder our purpose and passions, and whether life is unfolding as it should be. Travel links us to nature, to growth, and to introspection. When we connect with communities outside our own, it fuels resilience, self-confidence, and empathy for others; appreciation for diversity; and an openness to doing new things and being innovative and creative. Road trips allow us to embrace the unexpected, to take risks and push ourselves beyond our comfort zone. The road becomes a practice test for the metaphorical detours that we often need to take in life—and how we react to them. In essence, it tests how we react to uncertainties.

Remember those naysayers from chapter 2? One told me I shouldn't drive long distances as a woman alone. Well, I did just the opposite. I drove many times from Ottawa to Toronto and back in the same weekend. After my husband died, I started doing more road trips, and it was on those long stretches of road that I contemplated some of the most important decisions in my life and what I needed to do to move forward: everything from remarriage to career moves to saving and investing.

So far, my family has clocked over thirty thousand miles on road trips. We've done road trips in several different countries and states (from Dubai to Hawai'i). We also do "mini–road trips" if we take a weekend to travel.

When we journeyed from Ottawa to New York City, for instance, we passed through Washington, DC, and visited museums. For larger families (of five or more), road trips are often more cost effective than air travel. It was on a road trip from Las Vegas to the Grand Canyon, when we stopped at the Hoover Dam (known by some as the eighth wonder of the world), that my son Matthew exclaimed he wanted to be an engineer. The sheer awe the dam inspires, with its soaring concrete walls and, at the base of it, the water of the deepest hue of blue, brought the worlds that he had built with Lego bricks to life in a way that he never thought possible. It made him dream of building some of the world's largest structures.

ENRICH YOUR CREATIVITY WITH TRAVEL

Tim Ferriss wrote his book *Tools of Titans* while living in Paris to do a fiction-writing course.

Several of the entrepreneurs I interviewed for this book told me that their business idea or a life-changing mission happened on a road trip. Simply changing where we are can have a major impact on our level of creativity.

Greg Shepard, CEO of Dallas Maids, a cleaning company in Texas, took a month to travel Europe after graduating university. During the long train rides between destinations, he read. He asked three travelers he had bunked with on a train to Greece, "What's your all-time favorite book?" and he bought all three. This is where his love of reading started. Reading opened up a world of knowledge that has made his life rich beyond expectations. His passion for reading helped Shepard start his first of many businesses. It also helped him build a real estate portfolio. "The trip my parents gave me after graduating introduced me to a better education than I had received at university."

Similarly, musical saw–player Natalia "Saw Lady" Paruz (she plays the musical saw on movie soundtracks such as *Time Out of Mind* with Richard Gere, and she appeared in the film *Dummy* with Adrien Brody, among other credits) told me that after she was hit by a car, it was a trip to Austria that changed her life. She had been a professional dancer, and being hit by a car ended her career. Natalia explained that when she realized she was not going to be able to get back to dancing, she was devastated and "climbing the walls" trying to figure out what she was going to do with her life. Her parents wanted to cheer her up, so they took her on a trip to Austria because when she was a kid, her favorite movie was *The Sound of Music*. And it did; it changed her mindset, and now she is happily pursuing the life of her dreams.

Kristi Carlson, author of Amazon bestseller *Eat Like a Gilmore: The Unofficial Cookbook for Fans of Gilmore Girls,* based on the popular TV show *Gilmore Girls,* states that in September 2015 she spent six weeks as a tour manager on the road with her husband's band, Kicking Harold. During that trip, she quit her corporate job of seven years. It was during the long hours in the tour van that she researched and made the notes that ultimately turned into her first cookbook. Having the excess downtime on the road trip, when she really had nothing else to do, inspired her.

So, try what Kristi and others have done, and take a road trip somewhere that allows your creativity to explode like the cherry blossom trees in springtime in Washington, DC, and create worlds and ideas you never thought possible.

10

LIFELONG LEARNING (INCLUDING ANTI-RACISM AND GENDER EQUALITY)

An investment in knowledge pays the best interest.

—Benjamin Franklin

As women creating holistic wealth in our lives, lifelong learning will strengthen us individually and collectively; we're made stronger, healthier, wealthier, and more whole when *all* women have access to opportunities and education. The Law of Continuous Learning is critical to this lesson and to creating holistic wealth. The best way to put the Law of Continuous Learning into practice is for both individuals and organizations to recognize that education should be a lifelong endeavor, and should include robust anti-racism education to stomp out hate and oppression.

Lifelong learning is also associated with the Law of Abundance. Society tends to view human development with a scarcity mentality. Associated with a belief in limited resources is the belief in entropy—the breaking down, dissolution, or wasting away of an entity. When women re-enter the workforce after a period of maternity leave or caregiving in the home, they are labeled as having "skills atrophy" as a result. They return to work and are often given files that are less important, their direct reports are taken away, and their prior professional experience is stripped and negated, which leads to lack of promotions and salary increases over time. As a matter of fact, a study by Sandra Florian, a post-doctoral fellow in the University of Pennsylvania's Department of Sociology and the Population Studies Center, shows that women lose 5 to 10 percent of their wages for every child they bring into the world.[17] In response to COVID-19, more than 4.5 million women have had to leave the workforce because of childcare responsibilities. This could be catastrophic for women's economic security. On the *Holistic Wealth* podcast, author Eve Rodsky spelled this out clearly during our interview:

> We're at an inflection point, where if we don't learn from this crisis that it was completely unsustainable what we were doing to half of the population, then shame on us. . . . I will also say that every woman who listens to this has to recognize that we have our own agency.

---

17. Jacob Williamson-Rea, "Becoming a Mother Reduces a Woman's Earning Potential by up to 10 Percent per Child," Penn Today, November 20, 2018, https://penntoday.upenn.edu/news/becoming-mother-reduces-womans-earning-potential-10-percent-child.

Eve went on to describe her experience after going on maternity leave:

> What happened to me on my maternity leave was that I lost my direct reports. I started to feel even more eroded, because when I was in the office, I was being tracked, and when I wasn't there on maternity leave, I felt like I was being punished because my direct reports were taken from me. And then slowly and slowly, you feel like it's the death by a thousand cuts, to the point where you're forced out because of this . . . gross bias that you can't really put your finger on; and obviously this is much worse for women of color.

The "care economy" was worth $648 billion in 2019 (according to a new report by The Holding Co.),[18] but women's contributions are still not adequately factored in or recognized at the workplace or even in our earnings. The holistic wealth mindset needs to permeate our institutions and our organizations for systemic change to happen.

There's a general lack of perceived value for the enrichment of the human brain that is happening even when we are away from our desks. However, everything in life is intelligent, even nature, which forms our very existence. The universe is constantly evolving. When women create life and bring forth new human beings from their bodies, they receive an increase in cells, the very nature of existence; everything is symbiotic. But

18. "Care Economy Sized at $648 Billion and Poised to Grow Rapidly," PR Newswire, July 14, 2021, https://www.prnewswire.com/news-releases/care-economy-sized-at-648-billion-and-poised-to-grow-rapidly-301333403.html.

the notion of "skills atrophy" allows certain individuals to have control. This socially constructed view leads to inequality and poverty. It is a scarcity mentality that is highly oppressive for certain groups.

I believe that the single biggest threat to economic stability is wealth inequality and imbalances in the world. I also think one of the biggest threats is the issue of racism and systemic oppression. COVID-19 has exacerbated and highlighted the depths of the inequality in the world. As reported on Inequality.org, "since the formal beginning of the pandemic lockdown, the combined wealth of 713 U.S. billionaires has surged by $1.8 trillion, a gain of almost 60 percent. The total combined wealth of U.S. billionaires increased from $2.9 trillion on March 18, 2020, to $4.7 trillion on July 9, 2021." In addition, "one-third of [billionaires'] wealth gains have occurred during the pandemic."[19]

This is an important time in our history, especially as it relates to women, gender equality, racism, and social justice. In general, studies show that women continue to be disproportionately affected by economic insecurity. The *Global Gender Gap Report 2021* by the World Economic Forum (WEF) states: "As the impact of the COVID-19 pandemic continues to be felt, closing the global gender gap has increased by a generation from 99.5 years to 135.6 years." According to the WEF, as a result of the pandemic, in most countries, women are spending thirty-plus hours per week solely on childcare—almost equivalent to the average time spent at a full-time job. According to UN Women, globally, women are paid an average of 16 percent less than men.[20]

---

19. Chuck Collins, "Updates: Billionaire Wealth, U.S. Job Losses and Pandemic Profiteers," Inequality.org, August 23, 2021, https://inequality.org/great-divide/updates-billionaire-pandemic/.
20. "Everything You Need to Know About Pushing for Equal Pay," UN Women, September 14, 2020, https://www.unwomen.org/en

Black women make just 63 cents for every dollar a man earns, compared to the 82-cents-per-dollar wage gap for women of all races combined. In other words, a Black woman has to work until age eighty-six to make the same amount of money a man earns by age sixty. Black women earn about one million dollars less over the course of their careers. And it's even worse for Black working mothers, who earn just 52 cents for every dollar a man makes.[21] Furthermore, the coronavirus pandemic hit Black women the hardest. Black people are twice as likely to die from COVID-19 as white non-Hispanic people, and Black and Latinx women are experiencing job loss at higher levels than their white counterparts.

I have had my own professional experiences of racism as a Black woman even before the pandemic. I remember traveling on a work trip halfway around the world, in a historic capacity, at the highest level. I was the only Black woman present, in a group of mainly white men, and one afternoon while we were getting ready to embark on the second leg of our trip, we had a quick meeting while standing with our luggage packed and prepared at our feet. At the end of the meeting, one of the men—someone in a leadership position—looked at me firmly and, in front of everyone present, asked me: "Are you here to take care of the luggage?" Of course he knew full well my capacity there—we'd flown halfway around the world on the same flight. We had just finished working on a very high-level initiative together, one that I had crafted from scratch with my ideas and my brainpower. Yet in a split second, my purpose and role on the trip was brought down to handling luggage.

/news/stories/2020/9/explainer-everything-you-need-to-know-about-equal-pay.

21. Sharon Epperson, "Black Women Make Nearly $1 Million Less than White Men during Their Careers," CNBC, August 3, 2021, https://www.cnbc.com/2021/08/03/black-women-make-1-million-less-than-white-men-during-their-careers.html.

It dawned on me in that moment, as the others in the group stared at me in complete and deafening silence, that in other people's eyes, my worth as a human being was reduced to my skin color alone, regardless of my brainpower or the fact that I was there representing history. It reminded me of the film and book *Hidden Figures*, which shows how the Black women who stood at the forefront of innovation and history, pioneering new frontiers, had to stand in the background, humiliated and ashamed, our knowledge and brainpower stolen, and our purpose and role denied.

That day, my colleague was trying to erase history by rewriting my role and function. For the sake of generations after me, I will not allow it. I carried the weight of generations before and after me. Generations of Black women and men who have undergone systemic oppression and racism. What I have realized is that keeping silent can't change the world. Keeping silent can't change the future for our kids. The goal of sharing this story isn't to castigate anyone, but to invite everyone into the experience of minority communities so we can all learn and heal. There can be no holistic healing for some groups if there isn't an ongoing commitment and reconciliation. After the George Floyd protests, many organizations pledged to radically transform themselves with anti-racism ideals. We had high hopes of ushering in a new era—a sort of racial revolution—that would transform workplaces. One study recently pointed out that corporations pledged $50 billion to racial equity and have thus far spent only $250 million.[22] Another performative display of allyship that has yielded no results.

---

22. Michael Harriot, "It Turns Out, All Those 'Woke' White Allies Were Lying," *The Root*, May 24, 2021, https://www.google.ca/amp/s/www.theroot.com/it-turns-out-all-those-woke-white-allies-were-lying-1846959017/amp.

We will need to address issues of racism and gender economic inequality in order to have a better future. I believe that if we don't address these issues fiercely and urgently, we will be perpetuating a crisis of massive proportions that will be exacerbated by increased technological advancement and change. The vulnerable groups in society will be left behind. Women and children especially will suffer. We need significant and transformational anti-racism initiatives in organizations and in the workplace, coupled with accountability measures and strong actions against perpetrators who uphold racist ideals and block certain groups from achieving prosperity. Women need flexibility and support at work and equal pay.

At the Institute on Holistic Wealth, we have an entire module on anti-racism and gender equality. Certified Holistic Wealth™ Consultants, based all over the world, are engaging in community education efforts in their local communities and in organizations that serve teens and kids, like the Girl Guides and other community groups, as well as organizations that support entrepreneurs in growing and scaling their businesses. Holistic Wealth™ Consultants come from all backgrounds and industries and apply their skills and experiences to help their clients, and also to educate future generations. Every organization should have trained Certified Holistic Wealth™ Consultants embedded within teams and leadership structures. The Institute on Holistic Wealth is partnering with many organizations to do just this.

Our future depends on a generation that is equipped with the skills to move on from disruption. According to the World Economic Forum, some of the top skills needed for the workforce in 2025—such as analytical thinking and innovation, active learning, complex problem-solving, critical thinking, creativity, leadership, technology use and design, stress tolerance, and flexibility—are the very skills that can improve when disruptions force us to reinvent ourselves. But in order to foster these skills, we must make sure our education system is equipped with the right toolbox in advance of a crisis. The Holistic Wealth Mindset enables us to use disruption to our ultimate advantage. It's a framework for approaching challenges that schools could benefit from. Figuring out problems or issues that are often ill-defined and ambiguous, with vague solutions and an unclear pathway, will be important. Girls, in particular, who tend to shy away from STEM subjects and problem-solving, need to be reached in novel ways in the formal classroom. In March 2019, an article on the United Nations website indicated that despite a significant drive to reach gender equality, only 13 percent of girls are enrolled in STEM subjects.[23] Girls need to be empowered with negotiation and decision-making skills.

Women face massive penalties in the work world because of pregnancy and motherhood. It's like compound interest that never ends. If that little girl grows up and happens to lose her husband at a young age and has to take time off to take care of young kids, will she face a penalty when she returns to work? Will she be relegated to the back burner with a workload that isn't reflective of her skills and experience, punished because of a crime she did not commit? Will she have an opportunity to advance as a single mom with kids to take care of? Lifelong learning is vital for everyone—especially women and girls—because it opens doors and options for career transition, mobility, and growth.

Knowing this, combined with my own personal experience, I will never teach my daughter that there's only one kind of woman to be. While society tells boys that their options are endless, girls continue to be told by the media—and by some corporations that still don't embrace gender and racial diversity—that their world is limited. I will tell her that her

---

23. "Despite Progress, Companies Face Gender Equality 'Backlash,'" *UN News*, March 18, 2019, https://news.un.org/en/story/2019/03/1034891.

potential is limitless, and she should be bold and stand tall and courageously.

I will also tell her to demand the respect she thinks she deserves. I will tell her that her self-worth is not up for negotiation. She deserves to get the same pay as a man for the same job done. She deserves to be given recognition for her work and brainpower, as well as a fair chance for promotions and salary negotiations. She deserves to be given suitable learning opportunities to advance her career. She deserves to not pay a "mom" penalty in the workforce once she returns to work after having a baby. You know why? She is going to be the one to take care of her family—society, cumulatively—when her husband dies or if she becomes divorced. Is society empowering its little girls as much as we need to be? I don't think so.

I now look at my two boys differently, too. They, in turn, need to be prepared to look at girls differently. I will teach them to treat girls and then women as true partners. I will tell my sons that the women they marry may end up rearing their children alone one day. Is she empowered for that task ahead? Does she have adequate provisions for their family in case something happens?

In the realm of holistic wealth, lifelong learning is the currency used to stay relevant. And it doesn't involve just classroom learning (though that's vitally important). It's about educating ourselves and our children in a revolutionary way of thinking to bring about racial and gender equality at the individual, organizational, and societal levels. It is a tool for resilience when faced with difficulties.

To increase your own holistic wealth, consider what learning you might benefit from now to contribute to your ability to be resilient through life's inevitable challenges. In addition, contemplate what opportunities for education you might advocate for or offer to another, to the benefit of all.

11

THE WORD *NO*

It's easy to say "no" when there is a deeper "yes" burning within.

—*Stephen Covey*

My husband was at work the day he died. He stayed there all day, until 5:00 p.m. During that time, the tumor bled and bled. According to the doctors, he might have felt a tightness in his abdomen caused from the bleeding, but he wouldn't have felt any serious pain, because it would have been a slow drip of blood at first—instead of an avalanche. This would have been a good time for him to leave and go to the doctor—or even the emergency room—to check out the discomfort. Instead, he waited until evening, when the avalanche started, when time was against him. During the day, I spoke to him, and he had a line of colleagues outside his office, wanting him to check their work. The lining up of colleagues outside his office happened repeatedly over several weeks and months. He was a financial manager and a wiz at figures, so colleagues trusted his judgment. Some of the colleagues in that lineup were senior executives, with higher positions than himself. He mentioned to me that he felt stressed and exhausted. I don't think my husband was a workaholic, but he did value being indispensable to his employer. This was something he prided himself on, and he repeated it many times during his short but highly accomplished career. The COVID-19 pandemic has brought to light this issue of workplace expectations, and being present at all costs, bolstered by a "culture of captivity" (as Leslie Forde dubbed it) that has kept workers in their cubicles from nine to five. This is further exacerbated by workplaces lacking sufficient supports for self-care and the flexibility to get up and run if you feel like you are literally dying. Saying no is a critical tool.

If he had only said no to the line of colleagues, maybe he would have had more time. He ended up making a life-or-death decision at work, during a period of extreme stress and mental exhaustion. Many of us unknowingly make life-or-death decisions at work—under extreme levels of mental stress and panic. It's hard to be brave and make the best decisions when you're experiencing stress and exhaustion. Saying no isn't a sign of weakness—it's sometimes a sign of strength. My husband was one of the strongest people I have known, but sometimes we think time is on our side. Sometimes saying no may save your family, may save your marriage, may save your life—depending on the context.

During COVID-19 many employees have started to lift their voices to say no to oppressive work environments. It's no wonder at this stage of the COVID-19 pandemic that this great resignation wave has descended upon us. Many workers are dreading going back to the office full-time and giving up the flexibility of working from home. As I discussed on the *Holistic Wealth* podcast with *New York Times* bestselling author Eve

Rodsky, many people have learned that location freedom—and time freedom—is also part of their holistic wealth. This is one of the main reasons why I established the Institute on Holistic Wealth, with online courses such as the Certified Holistic Wealth™ Consultant Program and other courses to help people take control of their time and money, as well as an online membership platform to help members craft a life of holistic wealth.

How often have you said yes when you really preferred to say no? What did those times of saying yes cost you in wasted energy, money, time, or mental anguish? In a world desperately needing authenticity, we need to strive to be true to ourselves. When we are beholden to the views of others and become people pleasers, it disrupts our sense of self, makes us feel dependent on others for self-validation, and robs us of feeling truly independent. The word *no* is like an asset in a metaphorical bank account where our life's energy is the holding. Use it to save, and use it to earn a greater sense of yourself, what's important to you, and where you want to spend your time and energy.

Living a life true to yourself and having the courage to express your feelings will require mastering the art of saying no. This is borne out in the book *The Top Five Regrets of the Dying,* by an Australian palliative care nurse, Bronnie Ware: "The regrets touch upon being more genuine, not working so hard, expressing one's true feelings, staying in touch with friends and finding more joy in life."

Holistic wealth is about having an intentionally designed life, which includes being more authentic and true to the vision you have for yourself. This may mean saying no in a wide range of situations. Saying no to requests that are out of scope with this vision or could endanger your physical, mental, or even your financial health is important. Several of the regrets that Ware identifies above share the common element of having to say no. Say no to the demands of society; say no to feeling shy about expressing your feelings; say no to actions that will put your financial health in jeopardy.

SAYING NO AT WORK

Saying no at work can be tricky. When you have established a solid reputation and brand and become known for executing well on various projects and being a solid leader, the pressure can get even worse when you have to find an elegant way out.

Burnout, which can lead to anxiety and depression, is at an all-time high. According to the World Health Organization, the annual cost of depression and anxiety in the workplace is $1 trillion per year globally. The World Economic Forum estimates that the global mental health crisis could cost the world $16 trillion by 2030. We need to create safe environments in which people can take breaks. In choosing leaders, and as leaders ourselves, we need to emphasize skills like empathy, active listening, emotional intelligence, and resilience as vital skills. If you're not feeling safe to speak up at work when you feel sick, when you have given to your limit, what tools and supports do you need to find the courage to say no?

Tammy Gooler Loeb Coaching & Consulting advises that "to get positive results from saying no, it has to be stated in a way that offers something positive or forward thinking. Setting boundaries and an example to others can be a powerful way of using no to make an impact or inspire others. I am a big fan of the phrase 'Yes, and . . .' By using the 'Yes, and' you create a situation where people feel heard and will be more willing to listen."

Keli Hammond, owner of B Classic Marketing & Communications and author of *Craved: The Secret Sauce to Building a Highly-Successful, Standout Brand,* shared the following with me:

> As a woman in leadership, I used to have a really tough time saying no. I felt like I needed to prove myself worthy of the role I'd been placed in. As a Black woman, I felt even more of a responsibility to show my A-game at all times because I'd seen instances where colleagues had made digs and threw other minority women under the bus if they challenged work requests. Ninety percent of the time I was the only Black woman in the room, and I felt like I was a representation for all that would follow. So, I took on everything and eventually became so mentally and physically exhausted that I could barely keep my days straight. My productivity was negatively impacted because I was being pulled in so many different directions every day, and the stress affected my health.
>
> Now, as an entrepreneur, I need to constantly remind myself that saying no is okay. I've become very selective about the clients that we take on. In entrepreneurship, you naturally wear a lot of hats, so saying no is imperative to keeping yourself sane. I've learned that saying no is actually advantageous and necessary in order to see real success.

LET'S BUILD NEW BOUNDARIES IN A POST-PANDEMIC ERA

COVID-19 has ushered in an era of heightened self-care and the need to live even more intentionally by design. In fact, many of us created new boundaries during the pandemic. Some of us juggled homeschooling, working from home, and taking care of household responsibilities. Pre-pandemic, almost half of households were led by single or breadwinning moms. Parents have toiled away at invisible work at the office and at home for years—with the expectation that this should be the norm. We all need more predictability, flexibility, and ownership in how, where, and when we work, which is the core mission of the Institute on Holistic Wealth. Women need to advocate for themselves and ask for what they need in order to be accommodated. If the workplace does not have those core supports in place, then it's up to you to build a life for yourself—one that works authentically for you. Members of the Institute on Holistic Wealth have access to free resources to craft a life that works—an intentionally designed life that meets your needs.

When we learn to say no at work and in other areas of our lives, we contribute to the creation of a culture that values health and well-being over the bottom line. Incorporate the word *no* into your vocabulary more often, and notice how your reserves begin to fill.

BUILD YOUR LIFE PURPOSE PORTFOLIO

In Part I, I shared eleven life lessons to build your holistic wealth in the area of intentional life purpose:

1. Life, Well Lived
2. Life on Your Terms
3. A Personal Mission
4. Goals, with Wisdom
5. The Incomparable You
6. A Sabbatical
7. Life Within Each Moment
8. The Natural World Around You
9. Road Trips
10. Lifelong Learning (Including Anti-Racism and Gender Equality)
11. The Word *No*

Here are eleven actions you could take to increase your holistic wealth for a deeper connection to yourself, to the nature of life, and to resilience during setbacks. Some of the items on the list are simply questions for reflection. Know that looking inside and getting to know yourself better are the first steps of an intentionally designed life. Choose to do one, some, or all of the following:

1. Reflect on what having a life well lived would mean for you. Write it down, and also use it to help shape your personal mission statement (see number 3 below).
2. Reflect on any negativity in your life, whether from others (naysayers) or otherwise. Think about an affirmation to help you overcome negative comments and emotions.
3. Write your personal mission statement, drawing on your most cherished values and a vision for your legacy.
4. Write the short- and long-term goals that will help you realize your dreams.
5. Reflect on where you might be comparing yourself to others. Analyze the thought patterns. What might you say to yourself instead? Write down a statement, and use it as an affirmation for a day or a week.
6. What is your dream sabbatical? Write about it for twenty minutes.
7. Take a mindfulness meditation course or use a guided meditation at home. (There are many guided meditations available on platforms such as Apple Music.)
8. Go for a walk in nature, lean against a tree in a park or your own backyard, or look at pictures of a gorgeous scene from nature.
9. Take a road trip across the country, or simply on a nearby country road.
10. Identify an area of learning that would contribute to your financial, professional, or mental health.
11. Practice saying "yes, and . . ." or "no" to set a boundary at work—or anywhere else.

PART II

FINANCIAL INDEPENDENCE

12

YOUR PERSONAL FINANCIAL IDENTITY

> All your patterns and programs, and things you've picked up from society, from parental programming—all of these things are creating a perception of what you can and cannot do.
>
> —*Jena Sophia, from the* Holistic Wealth Podcast with Keisha Blair

Figuring out your personal financial identity is critical to learning how to move past life's challenges. You could very well hit a prosperity wall if you don't know your personal financial identity and don't know how to harness its strengths. After the first edition of *Holistic Wealth* was published, readers were coming forward during the initial lockdown of COVID-19 to ask me to help them determine their financial identities. They wanted to delve deeper into understanding their finances, especially during the pandemic, when people became anxious about money and wondered how to put their money to work—that is, how to invest, rebound, and recover from setbacks. So I developed the Personal Financial Identity Framework and a free Personal Financial Identities Quiz (currently available on the Institute on Holistic Wealth website). The quiz has also served as a survey on personal financial circumstances during the pandemic. Looking at the data has yielded amazing insights, especially when coupled with the interviews on the *Holistic Wealth* podcast, where all my guests have been revealing their quiz results and discussing how their financial identities impact their investing and spending philosophies. So far, more than a thousand people have taken the financial identity quiz, and during the COVID-19 pandemic, the quiz has shown that the majority of them identify as Minimalists and are aligning their spending with their values. Many have also identified as Risk Takers and Anxious Spenders, and a smaller number as Maximalists.

While developing the Personal Financial Identities Framework, I had an epiphany. I became financially independent at thirty-one, already having developed a multimillion-dollar portfolio, because I embraced my own personal financial identity and harnessed its strengths to be more self-aware, advocate for myself, and preserve my strengths. Right out of grad school, when I started my first job, I was already uncomfortable with the notion that having one source of income was the best way to go. That idea to me was inherently risky. I had this deep, nagging feeling that my life could be upended any minute because all I had was this one income stream—my salary. I knew that if I didn't follow the nagging feeling and figure out a way to invest and create passive sources of income, I wouldn't be living authentically—and true to who I was. Turns out I am a Risk Taker. Risk Takers think differently in terms of planning ahead. Risk Takers feel uncomfortable when they have only one stream of income, making them vulnerable to economic fallout. I later realized that my personal financial identity saved me from economic ruin after my husband died. I also realized that embracing this identity, a building block of my personal financial independence portfolio, enabled me to take the break that I needed to get through the trauma and the grief. Having a financial independence portfolio allowed me to overcome the fear of temporarily walking away from my job and title to take a one-year unpaid sabbatical. On sabbatical, my portfolio also sustained me while I undertook a path to holistic healing. During COVID-19, it also became clearer to me, after I sustained a back injury and had to take time to heal again, that having a toolbox and proper foundation in place is crucial to recovery from disruptions of all sizes. Your personal financial identity (the foundation of your financial independence portfolio) is that toolbox.

During my interviews, whether on the *Holistic Wealth* podcast or otherwise, many women told me that society taught them to play it safe in order to avoid losses. However, if we look at the Law of Abundance, then there's an unlimited supply of energy and abundance to create more. If you want to achieve success bigger than you have ever had before, you need to embrace your own personal financial identity. To truly live a life on your terms and achieve an intentionally designed life, you will absolutely need to know your personal financial identity and harness its strengths.

THE PERSONAL FINANCIAL IDENTITY FRAMEWORK

The Four Personal Financial Identities (the "Four Money Languages")

How do our actions influence our capacity to achieve holistic wealth? Self-knowledge is crucial. By pinpointing our personal financial identity, we can avoid making the same money mistakes as others, and we can identify the aspects of a particular situation that are causing us to succeed or fail. For example, the Maximalist may need more systems of external accountability to succeed but is also excellent at social interactions and in motivating others. The Anxious Spender/Investor may need more confidence boosters, positive affirmations, and knowledge of different investments, as well as a personal mission statement that clarifies goals.

WHY IT'S HELPFUL TO FIGURE OUT YOUR OWN PERSONAL FINANCIAL IDENTITY

There is no "best" financial identity: this is very personal to each of us, so this exercise isn't meant to figure out the "best" or "worst" financial identity. The most successful, wealthiest, happiest, healthiest, or most productive people aren't those from a particular financial identity, but rather they're the people who have figured out how to harness the strengths of their financial identity, counteract the weaknesses, and build holistically wealthy lives. With wisdom and knowledge from the Four Personal Financial Identities, we can make better financial decisions, understand our money motivations better, embrace our own strengths, use our time more productively, and suffer less stress.

The Financial Identities Framework is intended to help us understand ourselves more deeply, not to limit our sense of identity or possibilities. The systems of personal financial identities are very helpful—because they serve as a starting point for self-knowledge about how we relate to money and our financial decisions. The Financial Identities Framework isn't meant to confine us, or to assign a label that determines everything about us, but rather to call to our attention hidden aspects of our financial character. It allows for healing, empathy, and further strengthening of relationships when we apply it in the context of family or other relationships with friends, a spouse, and coworkers. It is also a very helpful framework for healing our money mindset and money blocks (including ancestral money blocks), so we can rewrite our own personal money stories.

The Financial Identities Framework has four main criteria:

- **Overall debt tolerance:** level of appetite in taking on debt when assessing financial decisions.
- **Risk profile:** level of appetite in taking on additional risk in assessing financial decisions.
- **Expectations of others:** willingness to yield to the expectations of others, like spending money to go out with friends.
- **Inner expectations:** the expectations we place on ourselves, like keeping our New Year's financial resolutions.

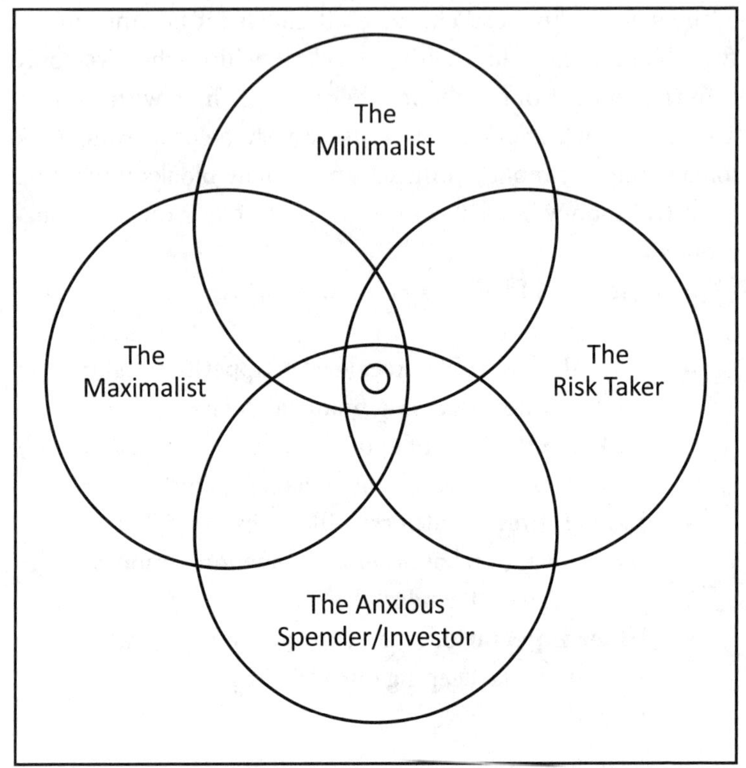

From the Institute on Holistic Wealth

THE MINIMALIST ("THE FRUGALIST")

Mantra: "Simple Living"

This person prefers to live life in simple terms and does not feel like they have to follow the crowd with their spending or investment habits. They are willing to take on minimal risk (on consumer spending) because their mantra is simple living at its core. The Minimalist satisfies inner expectations, and does not yield to the expectations of others, with either their spending or investing habits. This is a frugal person who can be astute with tracking spending as well as budgeting. The

Minimalist doesn't take on debt, and if they do, it is minimal, and they pay it back in full as soon as possible. Their appetite for spending on lavish things or just to show that they have reached a certain status is very low. When I think about a prominent Minimalist, Warren Buffett comes to mind, but I want to caution that not every Minimalist is exactly the same. With a net worth of over $90 billion, his debt and investment principles are sound. One of his principles is, essentially, don't ever get into debt unless you'll profit from it.

Minimalists won't spend just to fit into the crowd or be with the popular clique. Even if they climb the corporate ladder or succeed in business, their spending remains within their means. The Minimalist doesn't need flashy clothes, or cars, to prove their self-worth to others. Their appetite for lavish vacations is low, and they are content to just explore nature around them or engage in a hobby for fun. Fun doesn't have to mean additional spending. They are content and happy with what they have, and if they try out a new restaurant or dish that they like, they are happy just going back to the same place—because it's predictable and they know what they are paying for and that they will enjoy it.

When going out on a date, they don't need to be lavish or need lavishness from their partner. They are highly accountable for their decisions and don't need additional accountability mechanisms to follow through on their actions. The Minimalist will spend on things that are absolutely necessary and further their goals functionally. They tend to have strong impulse control and are the least impulsive of the four financial identities.

Signs that you're a Minimalist

- You prefer simplicity in everything.
- You don't feel like you need to follow the crowd with your spending or investment habits.
- You're willing to take on only minimal risk with consumer spending.

Strengths

Minimalists take on very little debt, live below their means, will not overleverage themselves, are very organized, have strong impulse control, and are thoughtful decision-makers. They keep strong financial records and track expenses.

Weaknesses

Because of their more conservative tendencies, they may take on less risk—which means less chance of loss, but also less potential reward. Others may view them as not very spontaneous (especially in dating or a relationship) because they track all their spending and tend not to go outside of their plan. They have a hard time spending money on themselves or loved ones.

THE RISK TAKER ("THE GOAL-ORIENTED SPENDER")

Mantra: "Goal-Oriented"

The Risk Taker prefers to take on more risk in an effort to accumulate more assets and investments, and with a view to furthering certain financial and lifestyle goals. They are meticulous at planning for big money milestones such as retirement or the birth of a child. Their risk-taking isn't fueled by self-indulgence but is goal driven. They prefer to hit certain money milestones by a certain age or life stage. They satisfy expectations about the life they envision for themselves, and to a certain extent they tend to shun the expectations of others in order to satisfy their need to accumulate assets and investments. This personality type prefers to plan ahead and plan well for the future. Risk Takers usually have an investment vehicle of choice, whether real estate, stocks, or something else, and channel their energies into accumulation of investments for the purpose of having a strong retirement fund or entrepreneurial endeavor.

Signs that you're a Risk Taker

- You're meticulous at planning for big money milestones such as starting a business or retirement.
- Your risk-taking is often goal driven.
- You prefer to hit certain money milestones by a particular age or life stage.

Strengths

Risk Takers are driven to learn new skills and are generally highly creative with their approach to finances. They are empowered to break through self-imposed limits to take risks.

Weaknesses

Risk Takers should beware their tendency to become overleveraged—with personal, business, or investment loans—and to take on more debt.

THE MAXIMALIST ("THE LAVISH SPENDER")

Mantra: "Go Big or Go Home"

The Maximalist or lavish spender has expensive tastes, but they also tend to have the biggest hearts in the room. They appreciate the beauty around them and have a desire to go above and beyond. If you're invited to a party hosted by a Maximalist, prepare to be dazzled—they will be the "host with the most." I've interviewed many Maximalists on the *Holistic Wealth* podcast, and they will go out of their way to make others feel special. They are fueled by having fun, and they enjoy the finer things in life and treat themselves to little luxuries every day. They are outgoing and prefer not to be burdened with tracking every last detail in terms of spending. Maximalism as a trend has received a lot of media attention during the pandemic, and especially during lockdown, because of TV shows such as *The Real Housewives* and social media accounts filled with glorious vacations, trendy interior design, and high fashion—all demonstrating an aspirational post-pandemic lifestyle.

The Maximalist's major weakness is the tendency to overspend, which can be detrimental to their financial future (that is, by getting them into debt). This personality type tends to need strong external accountability mechanisms.

Signs that you're a Maximalist

- You're the life of the party and you love making others happy—even if it means going over budget to do it (maybe a lot over budget sometimes).
- You like the best things or the most lavish things in life (like designer shoes), you drive an expensive car, and your home is *Architectural Digest*–worthy.

- Your Instagram feed is the envy of your social circle, and your vacations are lavish.

Strengths

Maximalists are fearless and energetic with a wealth of ideas. They are generous, enthusiastic, lovers of life, and the life of the party. They have a very active social life and social circles.

Weaknesses

Often impulsive and prone to succumbing to shiny-new-object syndrome, the Maximalist dislikes tedious record-keeping. Maximalists tend to be Risk Takers, have a propensity toward growing debt and can become overleveraged, are easily swayed to spend to impress others, and invest in lavish goods with depreciating value rather than longer-term high-yield investments. They tend to forget to plan for financial milestones such as retirement, and they struggle to track spending. A Maximalist needs strong accountability mechanisms.

THE ANXIOUS SPENDER/INVESTOR

Mantra: "Money Equals Stress/Anxiety"

The Anxious Spender/Investor is as the name suggests—a conservative, risk-averse personality, but with the added layer of also being worried about money issues and having a tendency to become anxious about making money decisions. This personality type is always worried about having enough for a rainy day and spends their life questioning, worrying, and feeling inadequate about their money decisions. Anxious Spenders can suffer from "analysis paralysis": endless research, anxiety, and worry about their money decisions. In order to overcome this problem, Anxious Spenders can give themselves a deadline or set limits when it comes to personal or business decisions. Another tactic is to find an accountability partner. The Risk Taker may be a great partner for the Anxious Spender due to their bold, courageous nature. From my interviews on the *Holistic Wealth* podcast with many Anxious Spenders, a spouse, partner, or friend was instrumental in helping them overcome their fears.

Signs that you're an Anxious Spender/Investor

- You're always worried about ending up poor or not having enough money for a rainy day.
- You question and feel inadequate about your money decisions.
- Your number one worry and concern in life is money-related.

Strengths

Anxious Spenders take on less debt and are therefore unlikely to become overleveraged. They tend to spend a lot of time saving and do not spend their income on frivolous purchases. This mindset allows them to take the time to discover their full potential.

Weaknesses

Anxious Spenders are concerned about their financial future. They worry about their lack of investment acumen to make decisions, so they have a tendency to avoid money or business risks in order to minimize mistakes. Because they take on fewer measured risks, they may overlook some beneficial personal, business, and investment opportunities.

MONEY MINDSET AND MONEY BLOCKS

In this book I've outlined several money blocks that get in the way of financial abundance and success. One of the major blocks to financial freedom is our money mindset. We've already covered some of the major money blocks to financial freedom like comparing yourself to others, equating net worth to self-worth, and a scarcity mindset. Ancestral money blocks can also influence our mindset. These are essentially false beliefs about money passed down from our ancestors that prevent us from achieving financial success.

In episode 29 of the *Holistic Wealth* podcast, I spoke with Jena Sophia about healing ancestral money blocks. Jena Sophia is a world-renowned subconscious specialist and healer who has worked with celebrities, Fortune 500 CEOs, athletes, and high-performers. According to Jena Sophia, "on a very energetic level, we are all connected to our ancestors." She goes on:

> The same eggs, for example, that were in your mother's womb, she was holding that life before you came. So you are actually absorbing the traumas, the perceptions, and the programs and patterns that came before you. So a really great place to start to try to figure out your ancestral money blocks is looking back at what your parents or caregivers were saying about money—what was the generation before that saying about money?—and really looking at the lineage of how money was talked about

> and related to how much you felt worthy of what you thought you could and couldn't do.

Jena went on to explain how the subconscious mind works in order to fully understand how these ancestral money blocks are passed down.

> If you think of an iceberg, and think about the very tip of the iceberg that you can actually see as being the conscious part of you, that is about five percent. Then there's this huge iceberg underneath: the subconscious, which is all your patterns and programs, and things you've picked up from society, from parental programming—all of these things are creating a perception of what you can and cannot do. So between the third trimester to the age of seven, our subconscious mind is being solidified.

HONOR YOUR OWN MONEY STORY

When you release money blocks and become self-aware about your own personal relationship with money, you can begin to rewrite your own personal money story. That process begins with knowing your own personal financial identity. I developed the Personal Financial Identities Framework based on this book, along with a free quiz to help you identify your own personal financial identity. (To try it for yourself, visit https://www.instituteonholisticwealth.com/take-the-quiz/.) This will enable you to start honoring your own money story and will help you identify your own money blocks to abundance (including ancestral money blocks). Figure out what money misconceptions you've embraced so you can figure out how you might be holding yourself back—and stop the cycle from repeating itself in your life. If money has been traditionally associated with feelings of trauma, guilt, low self-esteem, difficulty and challenges, and a general feeling of fear and panic, write down the triggers for these feelings and use the *Holistic Wealth Personal Workbook* as a journal to help you rewrite your personal money story.

Embracing your own personal financial identity allows for self-awareness, self-preservation, and self-advocacy. Whenever you feel anxiety, worry, or stress around a certain money decision, practice the Holistic Wealth Method, and start to think of your decisions as depletions or additions to your holistic wealth bank account. Use your personal financial identity to start rewriting your personal money story, and you will immediately start to feel a shift in energy and abundance.

13

FINANCIAL RESILIENCE AND RESOURCEFULNESS

We need to take agency in our own lives.

—Eve Rodsky, from the Holistic Wealth Podcast with Keisha Blair

Financial resilience and resourcefulness are two concepts that are critical to recovering from disruption. During COVID-19, *resilience* became one of the top buzzwords in the news. Financial resilience is the speed at which we can bounce back after a financial setback. Financial resourcefulness refers to how well we find ways to handle life-altering setbacks and maximize the resources we have. The way we mobilize and deploy our resources during times of hardship and disruption is key to overcoming those challenges. Resourcefulness means being smart with what we have in those circumstances—even if it doesn't feel like enough in that moment. For example, someone facing a job loss can compensate by exploring different income streams to bring in additional money.

YOUR PERSONAL HOLISTIC WEALTH PORTFOLIO

Financial resilience and resourcefulness need to be built into your personal Holistic Wealth Portfolio. I have been helping my coaching clients as well as training my Certified Holistic Wealth™ Consultants to make these considerations while financial planning. Your Holistic Wealth Portfolio also needs to be monitored over time, and its resilience measured with a score to help you identify weaknesses and vulnerabilities in your portfolio. The Institute on Holistic Wealth has developed a financial resilience score that can be assigned to your specific portfolio to test and measure its resilience. COVID-19 has shown us that ongoing stress-testing of our portfolio is critical. Traditional, pre-COVID financial advice recommended three to six months of emergency savings to cover your needs in the event of a setback. After weathering a global pandemic, it's clear that the old advice just doesn't hold true in a COVID world. At the Institute on Holistic Wealth, our recommendation is a minimum of six to nine months of emergency savings. Life insurance, another measure of financial resilience, is another area where traditional financial advice needs to change. At the Institute we recommend that families critically assess their life insurance needs.

One way to measure your current financial health is to consider allocative efficiency. Your resource allocation determines how efficient your purchases, savings, and investments are. If you allocate to primarily static investments—those with no yield or growth—then your allocative efficiency is weak. In order to have strong allocative efficiency in any Holistic Wealth Portfolio, it's necessary to look at your discretionary spending.

In other words, there are some classes of discretionary spending that do not contribute to financial resilience or financial resourcefulness. So the central question when examining your daily spending habits becomes: Will this item add to my financial resilience or financial resourcefulness? And if it doesn't—I think you know what to do.

CONDUCT YOUR ANNUAL HOLISTIC WEALTH REVIEW

An annual holistic wealth review will help you to increase your financial resilience and resourcefulness. It includes a status check of all the key pillars of your Holistic Wealth Portfolio, and it allows you to see where your weaknesses and vulnerabilities lie. It's a great exercise to do with your partner or spouse, or as a family (or even as a team). The Institute on Holistic Wealth has great resources for assisting you with this exercise and can help guide you.

Death or Divorce Check-In

A recommended part of your annual holistic wealth review is a check-in with your partner or significant other. When I interviewed author Eve Rodsky on the *Holistic Wealth* podcast, she had this advice to share:

> We need to take agency in our own lives because yes, there's all this bias—as women, we lose 5 to 10 percent of our wages for every child brought into the world. There's a lot of systemic issues that are really against women in terms of building wealth. And so our own agency is just asking those questions, not leaving it in the hands of a man. If

> you're married, really understand the family finances. We have our divorce check-in every year. I know this sounds very controversial, but it's our death and divorce check-in where we see what happens if he dies or if we get divorced, and we look through together what the legal documents are for his business. We go through all these scenarios together, and it sounds very strange, but it actually brings us closer together because I don't feel resentful, and I feel more at peace with how to control my future.

STRESS-TEST YOUR HOLISTIC WEALTH PORTFOLIO

Once you've completed your annual holistic wealth review and established an updated or "refreshed" budget, the key will be to stay on track. One of the best ways to accomplish this is to be well prepared for emergencies and disruptions, so that, when they occur, you don't have to reach for a credit card or throw your monthly spending plan entirely off course. This is a process that I call "allowing for contingencies." Stress-test your budget and ensure that there's enough wiggle room for emergencies. This will allow you to better stick to the budget that you've created for yourself.

CREATE YOUR PERSONAL MONEY MISSION STATEMENT

Your personal money mission statement can be a subset of your overall personal mission (as discussed in chapter 3). It should incorporate financial resilience and resourcefulness, as well as your personal financial identity (as discussed in chapter 12) and your personal money story. In crafting your personal money mission statement, think about the Law of Abundance, the Law of Continuous Learning, and the Law of Reciprocity (that is, giving back and advancing humanity). It will be aligned with the values that you've outlined for your overall mission. See the *Holistic Wealth Personal Workbook* for help with crafting your personal mission statement, or visit the Institute on Holistic Wealth, which has a great personal mission template.

14

A WELL-PLANNED FUTURE

Hold thoughts of wealth in our mind; the universe will return wealth to us.

—Napoleon Hill

Financial independence typically means having enough income to pay your living expenses for the rest of your life without having to work full time. Some people achieve this through saving and investing over many years, while others build successful businesses that can generate income without daily supervision. Holistic wealth is something to cultivate in many areas of your life, from enriching your sense of purpose, to nourishing yourself spiritually and physically, to creating good relationships and giving back. Developing in these areas helps us better rebound from setbacks. In the realm of finances, holistic wealth involves working toward financial independence, and several strategies will help propel you there.

Nothing is guaranteed in life. A whole life can be lost in minutes and can be wasted in the small moments missed. None of this is forever.

Luckily, we had a life insurance policy. Before my husband passed away, we sat down with a financial adviser to plan our future. We didn't know anything was going to happen; we actually were just looking at various retirement options. The adviser reviewed our portfolio and realized that with another child on the way, we didn't have enough life insurance, so we bought more. That was one year before my husband passed away. Now I take financial planning for the future very seriously.

Purchasing life insurance was the single most important financial decision we made. However, according to a 2021 report published by the Life Insurance Marketing and Research Association (LIMRA), only 52 percent of US households own some form of life insurance. One hundred and two million Americans say they need more life insurance. According to the report, the pandemic has increased the likelihood that many will buy life insurance: almost one in three (31 percent) say they are more likely to buy it because of the pandemic.[24]

For those who have a life insurance policy through their banks, it is usually woefully insufficient. This is therefore part of the training that I offer in the Certified Holistic Wealth™ Consultant Program. A life insurance policy taken out with your mortgage will only pay off the remaining balance on the mortgage. So, if you have a $40,000 balance, the bank will pay that amount. These life insurance policies do not cover funeral expenses, education costs, or other important expenses. Statistics also show that there's more than a 50 percent chance that one member of a couple will need long-term care. You need to build that into your planning process, too.

---

24. "2021 Insurance Barometer Study," LIMRA, April 12, 2021, https://www.limra.com/en/research/research-abstracts-public/2021/2021-insurance-barometer-study/.

Some insurance policies, like whole life insurance, are structured to act as an investment plan where you save funds that earn interest over a period of time and get paid out in lump sums. Depending on the insurance company, you could use this as a retirement benefit or even a personal loan.

For women who are single, widowed, divorced, or in times of job loss, we may wonder if we can also hold on to valuable assets such as real estate. Justin Pogue, author of *Rental Secrets,* has this to say about keeping your home during a life-altering setback:

> Those who were most successful in keeping their housing during a setback had a few things in common. They maintained their financial capital by keeping their expenses, including rent, lower. They communicated their situation well and developed relationships or social capital to call on when they needed it. Lastly, they focused on their next immediate goal instead of all the potential "what ifs," thus preserving their mental capital. Maintaining flexibility and reducing stress in these areas greatly improved their odds of success.

Pogue goes on to state that every spouse should develop a relationship with the professionals and companies providing services for the family investment portfolio, especially for any real estate. These relationships will be invaluable in helping the surviving spouse get up to speed quickly. If you own real estate, each rental property must be analyzed objectively. Is it profitable? Can it continue to be managed as it was in the past? Who would manage it if the deceased spouse self-managed? Are there better uses for the property, like renting rooms individually instead of renting it as a single unit? I would recommend seeking out business or real estate consultants to answer these questions.

Having an emergency fund with savings to last six or nine months is also ideal. An emergency fund can be a lifesaver in cases of long-term illness, a job loss, sudden death, or divorce. An emergency fund is a building block of financial resilience—which I've defined as the speed at which we can bounce back from setbacks or tragedy. Similarly, a life insurance policy and critical illness/disability insurance are all building blocks of financial resilience.

A well-planned future also starts with developing your own financial identity. One way to do this is through financial literacy. Improving your financial literacy is also the greatest stimulant of wealth. Many of us make our first large purchase with a spouse or significant other. The first house, the first car, the wedding and honeymoon—these are all expenses tied to our expansionary years. We therefore transition into adulthood not having gained a full sense of our own personal financial identity. For instance, what is my investment identity? What are things I will splurge on versus save on? This can also be tied to our values and mission in life. It is highly individual.

Each of us should have a financial identity—one that is distinct and separate from our spouse's or parents'. If you find yourself always wondering what your friends or parents think about the way you spend or invest, then it's an indication that you haven't fully figured out your financial identity. It's impossible to design a well-planned future without a proper financial identity—we end up living our lives in the footsteps of others—and possibly making the same money mistakes (see chapter 12 for more on determining your own financial identity).

Given that I was widowed at thirty-one, I firmly believe our twenties are crucial to forming the foundation of a well-planned future. Dear reader, if you have passed that decade, like I have: not to worry; there's still time. For those of you who read this and are still in that decade—make the utmost of it. According to Dr. Meg Jay, author of *The Defining Decade: Why Your Twenties Matter—And How to Make the Most of Them Now,* "how you spend your twenties will define you, as 70 percent of wage growth happens in the first ten years or so of your career." Dr. Meg went on to tell me that "contrary to the messages we receive from popular culture, one's twentysomething years are not a trivial, throwaway time but rather are a development sweet spot—a time when the small things we do and don't do (not just at work but in love and wellness, too) can have a great impact on our thirties and beyond."

According to a PayScale study,[25] "both men and women see salary growth of about 60 percent by age 30. After that, however, the rate of growth slows for women. By age 39, the typical woman's income has grown by less than 20 percent, compared to her 30-year-old self." Even though you may get cost-of-living raises along the way, the days of the double-digit raises will be long gone. The only thing that can make up for this loss is saving and investing for the long term.

Part of a well-planned future and achieving holistic wealth includes planning for the long term. Embrace estate planning by ensuring that you have a will or trust, especially if you have children (at any age). A full estate plan can also include your wishes in the case of health care emergencies.

It's never too late to learn how to manage your finances. But planning ahead for even the most unwelcome contingency, and even better, for financial independence, is a means of building in resiliency. Talk to a financial planner who can help you identify any other support you need to strategize for your future.

---

25. "Do Men Really Earn More than Women?" (infographic), PayScale, https://www.payscale.com/gender-lifetime-earnings-gap#methodology.

15

A PLAN FOR FINANCIAL LONGEVITY

Luck is what happens when preparation meets opportunity.

—Lucius Annaeus Seneca

We should plan for our longevity like the leaf-cutter ants. They are masters of the art of productivity. The leaf-cutter ants meticulously store reserves away for a rainy day. The colony is stocked and primed for long-lasting value. Looking at our savings, finances, and cash reserves like a colony that is intricate and built bit by bit is a good framework for financial resilience and planning for longevity.

Some of us will live to be a hundred years old or older. The average person can expect to live nearly thirty years more than someone born in 1900—almost to age eighty—and many people are living longer than that. Each person should do a careful assessment of their overall health, financial status, likely long-term care needs, and family longevity. For that, it helps to have a financial professional.

Here are some ways to plan for longevity.

PAY OFF OUTSTANDING LOANS ASAP

Once you pay off your loans, you won't have to worry about servicing steep monthly payments if you lose your job or face disruption through divorce or widowhood. Start with the high-interest loans first and then tackle the others. Another strategy is consolidating all your loans into one payment that is manageable and that allows you to get rid of it in the most efficient way possible.

FUND YOUR RETIREMENT SAVINGS

This is very important when planning for longevity, and if your current employer has a matching contribution, then that's even better. Even if a bout of unemployment forces you to dip into your retirement account, you'll likely come out ahead, because the matching contribution you collect could be worth more than any tax penalties you may have to pay.

GET A HOME-EQUITY LINE OF CREDIT

A home-equity line of credit could be a potential source of temporary cash in case of job loss or other financial setbacks. Even if you have a life insurance policy or emergency savings, you may need another type of financial cushion, and it's better to plan to have your bases covered. A home equity line of credit also typically has lower interest rates than credit cards or the average loan.

THINK TWICE ABOUT NEW FINANCIAL OBLIGATIONS

Planning for financial longevity means ensuring that you have a pot of money that won't run out. Taking on more financial obligations could put that pot of money at risk. Think through purchases big and small and the implications for your future of spending now. If you don't need a brand-new car, and buying one might jeopardize your plan for financial independence one day, delay that large purchase or get a used car that's within budget.

LOOK FOR SAVINGS IN YOUR HOME

Matthias Alleckna, an energy analyst at EnergyRates.ca, a price comparison website that helps consumers find low-cost rates for electricity and gas, noted in an interview with me that

> when it comes to significant changes in life, we should take the opportunity to review expenditures and plan for longevity. In order to live a practical life, we often add more services and subscriptions to our day-to-day lives, from cable TV and streaming services to phone plans and other bills. Check whether each service is useful and stop wasting money on things you don't use on a regular basis . . . One of the first steps toward financial certainty is to cut unnecessary expenditures. This certainly includes paying more attention to utilities;

whether electricity or natural gas, you can save a lot of money on energy by doing reasonably small changes at home.

Another overlooked money tip is to see renovations as investments. Be it an energy-efficient upgrade or any other home improvement, such efforts will save you money and time in the long term, which are two essential components for a balanced budget. Some changes at home, such as new insulation or new appliances, can be quite expensive. Yet, you can start with small steps, i.e., purchasing insulation kits for windows or even switching out an old thermostat for a smart one.

If you are in a transition either through death or divorce or another type of transition that may affect your finances, Cristina Briboneria, CFP, in our interview, suggests the following:

- You first want to review all your fixed and mandatory expenses; this could be expenses from day care costs, bills, and utilities to your mortgage/rent payment.
- In the event of death: Are there expenses that you can go without, or are there expenses that must increase because of the death?
- In the event of divorce: Can you split some of these costs? For example, day care for kids?
- The surviving spouse and each divorcee should reevaluate their long-term goals for retirement or sending their kids to college. Each person has to determine how much they personally have to save to reach some of those goals. Just because

a person divorces or a person dies doesn't mean that the other person doesn't want to retire.

- Everyone should also shop out all their insurance needs and benefits through work. You don't want to be overinsured or underinsured, so shop for the proper health, home, auto, life, and disability coverage. Make sure you have enough life insurance coverage on yourself; or decreasing life insurance coverage could also save some people money during the transition.
- Sometimes people who are going through a divorce may be required to maintain a certain level of life insurance.
- People will also want to review their wills and beneficiary designations. You want to make sure that your ex-spouse is not a beneficiary for your 401(k) (US) or RRSP (Canada). A beneficiary designation is a legally binding contract; if a person were to get remarried but their ex-spouse was still the beneficiary of their account, their ex-spouse would still get their retirement account.

Like planning for the future, a plan for longevity builds your resilience—and the resources you'll need for a long, fulfilling life.

16

MEASURED RISKS

Mentally strong people don't fear taking calculated risks. They know taking the right risks could be the difference between living an ordinary life and living an extraordinary life.

—Amy Morin

It is important to take measured risks to achieve certain goals. For instance, the decision to buy that first home or investment property, or even starting that business you've always dreamed of, requires taking measured risks. Achieving your goals also rests on the realization that not taking measured risks, or simply not taking action at all, is detrimental to achieving holistic wealth. However, many people let fear and doubt get in the way of taking measured risks. The naysayers and the comparisons we make with other people and their successes contribute to learned helplessness and a state of paralysis that we sometimes feel in our personal and professional lives. Sometimes more stress comes from worrying about taking that leap and making the "wrong" decision than actually executing it.

We can create so many fake constraints when we evaluate risks that we entirely confuse the real constraints with the fake ones. If we constantly create fake constraints every day of our lives, we deplete that holistic wealth bank account. The key to achieving holistic wealth from the perspective of taking measured risks is being able to let go of fear by perfecting the art of identifying fake constraints. As Caroline Jones Carrick, director of the TEV Project (an open innovation transportation project), states, "Every life has constraints. The hack is to know real constraints vs. fake ones, then work with them."

Becoming widowed at thirty-one, eight weeks after giving birth, is a real constraint. It ain't fake. However, as I learned then, with time even real constraints can be overcome somewhat by taking measured risks. It would have been easy for me to sit back after my husband died and not take any measured risks. If I had listened to the naysayers, I would have become paralyzed with fear. I was frequently frustrated with modern self-help books after becoming widowed. They often talk as if an individual is the only variable in an equation and so is devoid of constraints. Constraints are seen as a figment of the imagination. Well, some constraints are real and lasting. The good news is that you can take steps to learn how to properly identify real and fake constraints in every situation. Learning how to do so is key to achieving holistic wealth.

IDENTIFY REAL AND FAKE CONSTRAINTS

Let's look at some real and fake constraints so that when we think of taking measured risks, we're not confusing the two:

1. **Real Constraint:** Widowed at thirty-one, eight weeks after giving birth. This is a real constraint; however, it is a short-term constraint, not a long-term one.
2. **Real Constraint:** Discrimination and racism in the workplace. This has the ability to impede upward mobility of some groups and can lead to career stagnation and loss of income (through loss of salary increases over time, with no promotions).
3. **Real Constraint:** Gender inequality in the workplace and lack of pay equity. This isn't necessarily reflected in all organizations, but it is still a struggle writ large. In the case of pay equity for women, this becomes a long-term constraint and can severely affect income levels and the ability to bounce back from setbacks and adversity.
4. **Fake Constraint:** Thinking you can't grow your business because you have limited financial resources. While access to information may pose a barrier for some in terms of finding resources to grow a business, this is really a fake constraint. There are always ways to find resources, and it's not just financial resources that can help you grow a business.

Think of your own fake and real constraints, and think of how, in the past, you have overcome the ones which were real but only short term. What about the long-term ones? How can you implement strategies to overcome them to fulfill your purpose?

CONSTRAINTS ARE THE CATALYST TO CREATIVITY

We are conditioned to run with the status quo but not to resolve situations that cause ambiguity. The school system provides a very good primer on how to achieve the status quo and maintain it. The school system isn't very good at teaching the art of recovery from disruption, the art of becoming unstuck. One of the causes of "stuckness" is one's mindset: a scarcity mindset rather than a holistic wealth mindset fosters being stuck.

HOLISTIC WEALTH MINDSET

A person who approaches life with a holistic wealth mindset doesn't fear taking measured risks. The holistic wealth mindset does not erect fake constraints as barriers to success. People with this mindset are adept at recognizing fake versus real constraints, and they have mastered the art of recovery from disruption. They don't compare themselves with others—and they face crisis with dignity and grit. They view setbacks as only temporary—not a permanent constraint. They embrace a holistic wealth mindset that comprises not only financial savvy and independence but also elements like a life purpose and mission, spiritual connection, and a generous demeanor—all of which leads to a greater sense of wholeness and resilience in times of difficulty, as well as to happiness and joy. At a basic level, they integrate the aspects of holistic wealth in key aspects of their lives, including their finances, physical health, emotional and spiritual wealth, and wealth in their relationships with others, as well as contributions to humanity.

The holistic wealth mindset also calls for making decisions based on the Holistic Wealth Method: Will this decision be a withdrawal from or a deposit to my holistic wealth bank account? Approaching life with a holistic wealth mindset means approaching life mindfully and with the realization that each decision and each action represents a withdrawal from or deposit to that holistic wealth bank account. Repeated withdrawals from the holistic wealth bank account will lead to bankruptcy. Similarly, there are some actions that act like compound interest in a holistic wealth bank account, like listening to your intuition and lifelong learning—the benefits of these actions multiply over time in many different areas of your life. The Holistic Wealth Method can be applied in everyday situations regarding a range of daily decisions. For example, in assessing if a decision will add to your holistic wealth bank account, think about the vision of your life going forward and what you truly want for yourself. If you have toxic relationships that cause anxiety-provoking reactions, then ask yourself if keeping these relationships is a deposit into or a withdrawal from that bank account. Similarly, in thinking about your current spending habits, daily eating regimen, and the amount of time you spend on social media, examine how these actions add to (or take from) your overall holistic wealth. Holistic wealth is about having an intentionally designed life—so changing your mindset is key to ensuring you can achieve it.

GET UNSTUCK

Recognize when you are stuck in a particular mindset. Practice new behaviors by challenging constraints, assessing whether they are fake or real. Get creative to overcome constraints. You might focus on the outcome you want as a way of becoming unstuck. Then learn to say yes to your desire for achieving your goals, even if they involve risks.

Assess the risks, too. Consult with a professional if you need to, and decide whether the risk is worth it or not. For example, growing your business might not be worth it right at this moment if it could involve sacrificing your child's education fund. But it might be worth the risk if it means sacrificing money put away for the long term that you know, no matter what happens, you'll be able to recoup. Keep in mind that every risk is an opportunity waiting to happen (if executed well). The fear of taking calculated risks will rob you of mental strength—if you let it.

As psychotherapist and bestselling author Amy Morin states in an article on her website (www.amymorinlcsw.com), there are nine signs that you fear taking calculated risks:

1. You struggle to make important decisions in your life.
2. You spend a lot of time daydreaming about what you'd like to do but you struggle to act.
3. You make impulsive decisions because thinking about your options is just too anxiety provoking.
4. You think you could be doing more adventurous and exciting things in life, but fear holds you back.
5. When you think about taking a risk, you usually only imagine worst-case scenarios and choose not to take the chance.
6. You sometimes let other people make decisions for you so you don't have to make them.
7. You avoid risks in at least some areas of your life—social, financial, career, or physical—because you are afraid.
8. You base decisions on your level of fear. If you're a little afraid, you might do it. But if you feel really afraid, you decide it's unwise to proceed.
9. You think outcomes are largely dependent on luck.

Measured risks are an aspect of holistic wealth that includes financial versatility. They are catalysts for movement, growth, and change in our lives. They signal not only courage to act in the face of uncertainty, but also a measure of confidence in managing financial risk.

17

A SOLID LONG-TERM INVESTMENT

> There is a tide in the affairs of men which, taken at the flood, leads on to fortune; omitted, all the voyage of their life is bound in shallows and in miseries.
>
> —*William Shakespeare,* Julius Caesar, *act 4, scene 3*

Warren Buffett, Benjamin Graham (a.k.a. "Father of Value Investing" and "Dean of Wall Street"), and Seth Klarman all believe in investing for the long term. They also believe in value investing. In *Wealthy by Design: A 5-Step Plan for Financial Security,* Kimberly Foss, CPA, CPWA, states, "If you were to have purchased Berkshire Hathaway stock originally at $12 per share, you would own stock worth well over $133,000 per share today."

Investing is part of a solid retirement strategy. Learn all you can about your chosen investment, and dive in. Don't get into debt or leverage what you don't have, but take a measured approach to investing and stick it out. Make sure you invest in something you truly love. I've always loved real estate, and I found that after my husband died, investing in real estate gave me some amount of financial stability so I could spend more free time with the kids.

INVESTING IN REAL ESTATE

My brother, Donald, got me interested in real estate. When he was a university student of about twenty years old, he started a taxi service and hired a driver to run it, and then he used the income from the taxi service to start buying real estate. Little by little, each year he acquired yet another rental property, until he had a portfolio of houses, condos, and then commercial properties. These investments enabled him to achieve financial independence much younger than his peers and also offered a retirement cushion in later years.

My friend Angela Singhal in Ottawa is the executive vice president of Richcraft Homes, a family-owned, thirty-five-year-old real estate development, construction, and property management company. Founded by Kris Singhal, Angela's father, Richcraft has grown to become the largest private landowner in Ottawa, with over fifteen thousand homes, and over 1.4 million square feet of industrial and commercial buildings.

Angela shared with me the following thoughts:

> As an immigrant from India with an accounting and law background, real estate wasn't on my father's radar until he sold my mom's home for a profit, and then a light bulb went off. Real estate makes good business sense in the short term, but only if there is some additional value you can bring to the property in the period

> between when you take it off the market and when you put it back on the market. So, take a vacant infill lot, for example; you build a house, and sell it. Or take an existing house, fix it up, and then flip it. You've created value on that property, but only if you can sell it for more than what you spent to build or fix it, and if it is worth your time. Otherwise, real estate investment needs to be a long game: you live in the home yourself, you rent it for positive cash flow, or you own some land and wait for it to increase in value. And it will. Historically, real estate has always gone up in value, if you are willing and able to hang on. Avoid the pitfalls of being house poor. Mortgages, taxes, insurance, and carrying costs need to be proportionately small relative to your income. A good rule is generally 25 percent of your income should be budgeted for these costs of ownership.

On the *Holistic Wealth* podcast, I had an opportunity to sit down with Malena Crawford, author of the bestselling novel *A Fistful of Honey* and founder of the Black Divine Feminine Reawakened movement, a Facebook group dedicated to empowering Black women that has more than seventy thousand followers. Malena is also a Certified Holistic Wealth™ Consultant. She's a six-figure-earning coach and real estate investor who is passionate about the benefits of real estate investing for empowering women. On the podcast, we discussed tips and strategies for investing in real estate with little to no money for a down payment, like investing in small cap properties worth $30,000 to $50,000, house hacking (i.e., renting part of your current residence for income), and partnering with someone else to invest in real estate. During the first part of the COVID-19 pandemic, in May 2020, Malena took a risk and bought a multi-unit investment property that's now worth much more in value because of the demand for housing and low inventory.

Real estate as a long-term investment can help build a portfolio of passive investments. Real estate can also offer a buffer in retirement and help build up that holistic wealth bank account.

VALUE INVESTING

For an investment to be a good one, it has to be priced attractively so you can get a return. This is the core principle of "value investing." Keeping your long-term goals in mind when you make choices about where to invest your pot of money will yield more efficiency and success.

Robert R. Johnson, CFA, CAIA, coauthor of *The Tools and Techniques of Investment Planning, Investment Banking for Dummies,* and *Strategic Value Investing*; professor of finance at Heider College of Business, Creighton University; and chairman and CEO of Economic Index Associates, stated the following in my interview with him for this book:

> Building wealth is a marathon, not a sprint. A long-term perspective is the single most important quality necessary for success in investing. The reason is that markets can be irrationally overvalued or undervalued in the short term. Benjamin Graham, the father of value investing and mentor to Warren Buffett, explained the concept of value investing by saying, "In the short run, the market is like a

voting machine, tallying up which firms are popular and unpopular. But in the long run, the market is like a weighing machine, assessing the substance of the company." Sentiment drives the market in the short run, while fundamentals drive the market in the long run.

Long-term investors should have a diversified portfolio of common stocks and ride out market volatility. According to data compiled by Ibbotson Associates, large capitalization stocks (think S&P 500) returned 10.2% compounded annually from 1926 to 2017. Over that same time period, long-term government bonds returned 5.5% annually and T-bills returned 3.4% annually. The surest way to build wealth over long time horizons is to invest in a diversified portfolio of common stocks. To that point, an old Wall Street proverb states that "Nobody rings a bell at the top or the bottom of the market." Investors are well-served to ride out the volatility and not attempt to time the market.

Investors who get in and out of the stock market invariably end up buying high and selling low. Even missing a few positive days can negatively impact your return over a long period of time. From 1996 through 2016, the S&P 500 returned 8.19 percent annually. If an investor attempted to time the market and missed the five best days, her return would fall to 5.99%. While it is true that long periods of time can witness anemic returns in the stock market—the lost decade of the 2000s witnessed an average annual return of –0.9% on

> the S&P 500—since 1970 the lowest twenty-year holding period for large cap stocks provided a return of 7.20% annually. The best way for the novice investor to accumulate wealth is to invest in the stock market and hold for a long period of time. Remarkably, $1.00 invested in a large capitalization stock market index at year end 1925 would have grown to $7,352.68 by year end 2017.

Benjamin Graham, quoted in Robert's text above, was a mentor to Warren Buffett. In Robert Johnson's book *Strategic Value Investing*, the authors noted that Warren Buffett calls *The Intelligent Investor* (written by Benjamin Graham) "by far the best book about investing ever written." *The Intelligent Investor* highlights one of the key investment lessons at the core of investing: diversification is a key component of investment strategy. When Robert Johnson reached out to Buffett to get textbook recommendations for his finance course at Heider College, Warren Buffett personally recommended *Security Analysis* and *The Intelligent Investor*, both by Benjamin Graham, and *Common Stocks and Uncommon Profits and Other Writings*, by Philip Fisher.

During the course of the long-term investment, depending on your risk tolerance, you will encounter volatility. How you react to this volatility will determine the success or failure of your long-term investment. If you change your portfolio allocation when facing volatility, you will not obtain the returns on your investments over the long term. There is the danger of buying high and selling low. If you can stick to the allocation, you're more likely to obtain those positive returns. Therefore, it's very important at the start to have a portfolio that matches your risk tolerance. In this way, investors will not react and make decisions which will impact their portfolio negatively.

This is another reason why knowing your personal financial identity is important. Visit the Institute on Holistic Wealth website to take the free Personal Financial Identities quiz, in order to fully understand your risk tolerance.

While I cannot advocate for investing in one instrument over the other, I can suggest that you do your research, analyze your goals, consult with a financial expert if you need to, and then choose a long-term investment that best meets your vision. This is a holistic approach to building wealth. Investing for your future is an essential part of financial planning and being able to "weather the storm," should there be a disruption in your life, and a measure of financial literacy will help you make the right choices for you. It is also a critical piece in building that holistic wealth bank account.

18

FREEDOM FROM DEBT

A man in debt is so far a slave.

—*Ralph Waldo Emerson*

I got married in December 2001, during what was then the worst market crash since the Great Depression, with US stocks losing 50.2 percent of their value—or $7.4 trillion—between March 2000 and October 2002. Then, seven years later, my husband died at the height of the global financial crisis in 2009. Our seven years of marriage were sandwiched between two of the largest global economic crashes in history, and a period known as "the lost decade" between 2000 and 2009. During COVID-19, we once again encountered one of the most dramatic stock market crashes in history in March 2020. In four trading days, the Dow Jones Industrial Average plunged 6,400 points. Throughout my adult professional working years, I have now navigated through the dot-com bubble, the 2001 market crash, the 2009 global financial crisis, and the

2020 COVID-19 market crash. With each economic crash, I experienced a significant personal milestone as well: marriage, giving birth, the death of my husband and returning to work widowed, and then suffering a back injury. We live in an era of disruption—one in which we may face another "lost decade" at some point in the future. A key takeaway is that long-term investing is historically a winning strategy, as is having low debt.

Luckily, at the point my husband died, we had little to no debt. One of the things you don't want to have to deal with is having your life upended by death, divorce, a critical illness, an accident, or a job loss, and at the same time have to deal with a mountain of debt. That would be like Sisyphus with cash-flow problems. After Garfield died, I was constantly aware that I was now the main breadwinner. I wondered what I would have done if I had a ton of debt. Even without debt, the thought of it was enough to make my stomach churn. On top of the costs of living and raising two children, in the short term, I had funeral expenses to deal with. Even though we had life insurance, it wasn't processed for nine months. (Yes, it can take that long!) Funerals can be expensive, especially if the entire family has to travel out of the country. Imagine the stress of a person who has a pile of debt and has to borrow for a funeral, and so add even more to her debt.

Holistic wealth is about creating circumstances in your life that allow you to be resilient and resourceful. This will help you to renew as best as possible, when and if tragedy strikes. In this light, paying off what you owe—whether it's student loans, your mortgage, a car loan, a credit card, or another kind of debt—is always a good thing. I'd like every woman to have the goal of becoming financially independent, and being debt-free is an essential ingredient of this.

In the inaugural episode of the *Holistic Wealth* podcast, I interviewed Rachel Rodgers, CEO of Hello Seven and author of the book *We Should All Be Millionaires*. Rachel's story certainly reflects recovery from disruption after a setback. During the 2009 recession, Rachel faced a setback after her clerkship ended and she lost her job. Rachel described the circumstances in her *Holistic Wealth* podcast interview:

> I technically lost my job because it's a year term and then you're done. I was able to get unemployment benefits, which was allowed during that time. They kind of loosened up the rules. If you were starting your own business, you could get unemployment benefits, because we were in the middle of the great recession in 2009 and 2010. And so I was able to get some unemployment income, which helped to supplement my income. I moved out of my house and rented it out, and moved into a tiny little basement apartment with my husband. I got rid of my nice car and got a janky little Altima that cost me $800. I seriously downsized my lifestyle so that I could live off of a lot less temporarily so that I could start this business. So there was definitely some sacrifice there. And my startup costs were $300. The only thing I spent money on was professional liability insurance, which you need when you're practicing law, and business cards. . . . I used my laptop that I had from law school, I had a law degree, and I passed the bar, right? I was licensed to practice law. So I was the business, I really was just selling my own services directly. And so there weren't a lot of startup costs. And I recommend that. Even if you want to sell a

> product, if you don't have the capital, you can sell services.

Rachel hit a major entrepreneurial milestone in June 2020, when she brought in $1 million in revenue through her business coaching and membership community, Hello Seven, which subsequently increased to $2 million. She more than doubled her revenue to $5 million during a global pandemic. Some of the lessons immediately after her setback include significantly downsizing and keeping her expenses very low.

Paying off debts requires a financial strategy—and often sacrifices in service of freedom. Ms. Mod, who runs the Modest Millionaires website and is a thirtysomething parent from Quebec, Canada, told me that she and her husband outlined a goal to pay off their mortgage in five years. They took many steps to achieve this and surpassed it by a full year when they made their final mortgage payment almost exactly four years after they had taken out their $150,000 mortgage.

The main strategies that allowed them to pay it off in such a short space of time were buying a home at a price they could afford; having a flexible mortgage, one that they could pay off without significant penalties; making additional weekly payments; and using a high-interest, tax-free savings account to accumulate additional savings tax-free and then applying them to the mortgage balance.

Another blogger I spoke with, Emilie Cleaver of Wise Mind Money, is an Ohio-based millennial who blogs about paying off student loans and being intentional with money. She is still paying down her own student debt after graduating in 2016 and owing $78,000 in student loans. Combined with her husband, they had $108,000 of student debt as of August 2016. On the salaries of a teacher and a social worker (never more than $40,000 a year, respectively), in two years they had paid down more than $26,000 of the loans and another $9,000 in interest.

To do this, they had put their extra money at the end of each month toward the debt. Seeing the numbers go down fast motivated Emilie and her husband to cut unnecessary items out of their budget (they rarely buy clothing or eat fast food, for example) and find ways to make extra money (nannying a few hours per week, teaching a class, and doing small jobs).

Estimates suggest that the average student debt in Canada is now past the $28,000 mark for a bachelor's degree. The Canadian University Survey Consortium surveyed more than 18,000 graduating university students from thirty-six Canadian universities for its 2018 annual report. The average debt-ridden student owed $28,000.[26] In the United States the average student debt is $32,731, according to the Federal Reserve.[27] Winning scholarships can be part of a strategy to lower the cost of tuition and to graduate debt-free. One student I know, Kristina Ellis, otherwise known as the College Ninja, applied for and won more than $500,000 worth of scholarships—she didn't end up using student loans. Her first book, *Confessions of a Scholarship Winner: The Secrets That Helped Me Win $500,000 in Free Money for College—How You Can Too*, encourages students to approach each scholarship application like a salesperson, and it is a great resource for young people looking for ways to reduce the amount they need to borrow for that essential higher education.

The two cases above (Ms. Mod and Emilie) highlight strategies that can be applied to anyone and can result in not only

---

26. Cameron Yee, "Financial Aid Guide for University and College Students in Canada," *MoneySense*, December 2, 2020, https://www.moneysense.ca/save/financial-aid-guide-for-university-and-college-students-in-canada/.
27. "Report on the Economic Well-Being of U.S. Households in 2016 - May 2017," The Federal Reserve, https://www.federalreserve.gov/publications/2017-economic-well-being-of-us-households-in-2016-education-debt-loans.htm.

debt repayment but also achieving financial independence sooner. Steps like *living below your means*—through buying a home at a price you can afford or downsizing; having a flexible mortgage, one that you can pay off without significant penalties; making additional weekly payments to loans; and using a high-interest savings account to accumulate additional savings to pay off other loans—are sound strategies. In addition, having *multiple sources of income* works well for making additional payments to loans and generating savings, as does cutting out additional unnecessary spending.

FOCUS ON THE HOLISTIC WEALTH MINDSET

While being interviewed on the *Holistic Wealth* podcast, Malena Crawford, whom I first mentioned in chapter 17, talked about how childhood homelessness led to depression and negative feelings of self-worth and shared how she shed the victim mindset. Dr. Deana Stevenson, founder of Doc Deana Enterprises and Certified Holistic Wealth™ Consultant, also spoke on the podcast about overcoming her imposter syndrome on the road to starting her highly successful business. Dr. Stevenson now has a seven-figure education consultancy business.

For these entrepreneurs, cultivating a mindset that empowered them to achieve their goals was paramount. Malena Crawford now has a six-figure real estate and coaching business. These successes point to how mindset and positive mental health can play a crucial role in entrepreneurial success.

For small business owners, there are also strategies to reduce, avoid, and pay off debt. Entrepreneur Naomi Sinead Roopchand, CEO of Naomi Sinead Beauty, used funds from the sale of one business to invest in her next enterprise. As the owner of an online shopping service for women to buy, sell, and trade high-end dresses, she paid off a total of $27,000 over approximately two years, then managed to stay debt-free by reinvesting all her money into her business. After selling her website, she used some of the money to start the DermAesthetics Institute, which launched in November 2018. She stayed debt-free by not overleveraging herself and by taking baby steps in her industry. She changed her work attire to wearing $40 scrubs instead of the newest outfit from Saks Fifth Avenue. If she needs to take a course to help her career, she asks one of the salons she partners with to cover half of the cost, to help her grow both businesses. She needs to continue building her brand, so she downsized her home; instead of living in the city of Philadelphia in a high-rise apartment, she moved outside the city and pays significantly less. Last but not least, Sinead told me in an interview, "I stopped blowing my money on going to happy hours and events that were costing me money to socialize. Now, I only go to events/seminars that help me network and learn, because I can write them off in my taxes."

If you currently have debt, use the examples above to ignite your creative thinking about ways to reduce it and pay it off. Freedom from debt will pay back in scores of holistic wealth.

BUILD YOUR FINANCIAL INDEPENDENCE PORTFOLIO

In Part II, I shared seven life lessons to build your holistic wealth in the area of financial independence:

1. Your Personal Financial Identity
2. Financial Resilience and Resourcefulness
3. A Well-Planned Future
4. A Plan for Financial Longevity
5. Measured Risks
6. A Solid Long-Term Investment
7. Freedom from Debt

Below are five actions you could take to increase your holistic wealth in order to have a well-planned future. Some of the items on the list are simply questions for reflection. Know that sticking to a solid long-term investment, planning for financial longevity, getting out of debt, and taking measured risks are the first steps of achieving financial independence. Choose to do one, some, or all of the following:

1. Write down what a well-planned future would look like for you. Include long-term financial goals such as retirement.
2. Think about your approach to taking measured risks. Write down some real constraints and

analyze them. Make a list of constraints that stand in the way of your goals, and make a plan to overcome them.

3. Think about some ways you have taken measured risks. Have they contributed to your goals? What other risks are necessary for you to take to achieve them?
4. Identify a solid long-term investment that you would like to undertake. What is needed for you to take that step toward achieving it?
5. Think about your total debt. Are you taking extra steps to pay it down?

PART III

PHYSICAL AND SPIRITUAL NOURISHMENT

19

SPIRITUAL SELF-RENEWAL

An unexamined life is not worth living.

—*Socrates*

Spiritual self-renewal is about taking time to rejuvenate, letting the past go so a new you in a new phase of life can be born. This is a very powerful thing.

After my husband died, I felt like I was constantly harboring something I refer to as "dry bones"; these are things like fear, doubt, regrets, worry, the things I should have done, the symptoms I should have picked up on earlier, thoughts like "If only I had questioned the doctors more, maybe things would be different." I went on and on, around in circles, again and again. I learned the hard way that the only way to reinvent myself is to practice constant self-renewal. I had to let my old self die in order to make way for a rebirth. I took a personal inventory to see how much time I gave to these dry bones. It turns out I was robbing my future by harboring dry bones of the past.

The thing is, if we don't lay the past to rest, our lives will become like a tumbleweed that keeps picking up old hurts with the new ones that come along, until we're carrying so much that we can't move forward. C. S. Lewis, in his book *Surprised by Joy: The Shape of My Early Life*, writes, "All my acts, thoughts, and desires were to be brought into harmony with the universal spirit. I examined myself with a seriously practical purpose. And there I found what appalled me: a zoo of lusts, a bedlam of ambitions, a nursery of fears, a harem of fondled hatreds. My name was legion." Just as author Anne Lamott did, I too felt elated and absolved the first time I read this. C. S. Lewis had dry bones. Different ones, but dry bones nonetheless. On a certain level, we all have some.

As religious leader David O. McKay is quoted as saying, "The greatest battles of life are fought out daily in the silent chambers of the soul." If you win the battles there, if you settle the issues that inwardly conflict, you feel a sense of peace, a sense of knowing how you can set the direction of progress in your life—and this invaluable asset of holistic wealth is remittance for the hard, rewarding work of going inward to discover your true calling. Motivation from Within holds the keys to unlocking your purpose and setting a new direction.

We all go through valleys and peaks, but oftentimes those valleys can seem unpassable and the mountaintop an insurmountable, faraway dream. Many of us get stuck in our valleys, while some of us can make it back to the mountaintop more agile, better than before, and ready to take on the next challenge.

What makes the difference between those who have more mountaintop moments and those who seem stuck in the valley?

Without continuous, methodical, conscious efforts to renew ourselves, we can become stuck in the "valley of dry bones." The Law of Spiritual Self-Renewal is clear here: we must examine ourselves if we are to find our purpose and live a meaningful life—a life of greatness.

What I have termed the *Four Laws of Spiritual Self-Renewal* are critical to reclaiming your mountaintop.

#1: TAKE A PERSONAL INVENTORY

The very first step in taking a personal inventory is to survey your valley—are you standing with mostly dry bones? That failed relationship, divorce, death of a loved one, business that failed, or the career that never took off? These can physically, emotionally, and spiritually consume our very existence and block any hope of self-renewal or personal growth.

A personal inventory that explores our deepest thoughts will bring these issues to light:

a. **Negative Thoughts (Harboring the Valley):** How many of our days are spent harboring negative thoughts that block opportunities and blessings?
b. **Lack of Gratitude:** How much of our day is spent pitying our personal situation with little thought or recognition of the small blessings that have happened?
c. **No Forgiveness:** How much have we really forgiven ourselves and others for past hurts and missed opportunities?
d. **Misplaced Priorities:** How much of our attention and effort is placed on actually achieving our goals?

Prayer, meditation, and tuning in to your intuition are key in setting the direction in your life.

#2: SET THE DIRECTION OF PROGRESS

Many great leaders, such as Martin Luther King Jr., are considered great because they did something almost no one else believed possible—they literally set the direction of progress for generations to come. They didn't focus on just having a career or a job; they had a vision and a mission. For spiritual self-renewal, it is critical to refocus and set the direction of progress in your life. A new commitment to new priorities will also help keep hope alive.

Setting the direction of progress is the act of setting your goals and vision for your life. However, this isn't about attaining position, fame, and power as the be-all and end-all. As we will see, from a perspective of holistic wealth, goals should embody service to humanity and making the world a better place.

#3: RENEW HOPE AND MOTIVATION

Hope and optimism drive us forward to achieve our goals. Fierce optimism that can withstand all shocks, all mistakes, and all barriers is needed for self-renewal. It is standing in the face of relentless obstacles and finding a pathway to succeed. Many extraordinary individuals employed fierce optimism above all.

Winston Churchill is famed for keeping hope alive for the Western world in the early days of World War II. Similarly, Martin Luther King Jr. kept hope alive for millions of his followers, mostly in churches in the South, against systemic racism. He did this by setting the sights of his followers on a better day. He helped them imagine a land where "people were not judged by the color of their skin, but by the content of their character." He kept their hope and motivation alive even while they lived through some of the cruelest injustices in human history. They faced lynching, tear gas, horses, dogs, and guns. Regardless of those obstacles, they still turned out in droves to listen to Dr. King in order to renew their hope and motivation. This is one of the most prominent examples of the Law of Spiritual Self-Renewal in action.

These great leaders had dreams much broader than themselves—their goals were bigger than generations after them could have imagined. Their hope and optimism led to some of the greatest movements of our time and transformed humanity to become better, stronger, and more resilient.

#4: SPIRITUAL TRANSFORMATION

Spiritual transformation is fueled by a growing awareness of the reality of the soul: there is a conscious commitment to a life of self-discipline and active service in the world. Spiritual disciplines such as meditation, study, and service become habits of daily living. Spiritual qualities such as compassion, wisdom, and inclusive love take center stage. Spiritual self-renewal means relinquishing your old limited identity and becoming something more expanded, powerful, and closer to your true self.

Spiritual transformation is not enchained by what others think—or society's dictates about what encompasses success (e.g., money, job title, and so on). With such a transformation, the focus of your life has gone through an evolution—it's not focused on the valleys anymore; it's now focused on the mountaintops through serving humanity and achieving happiness in the now. The transformed soul asks, "What can I give to humanity?" rather than "What can humanity give to me?"

A NOTE ON FORGIVENESS

Forgiveness is also a critical part of spiritual self-renewal. After I became widowed, some of the negative comments I got from the toxic naysayers and others really threw me for a loop. They ranged from "No one will ever want you again with two kids" to, basically, "Your kids will never be happy again." I had to really dig deep, not only to prevent myself from lashing out at others, but also to forgive. I never had a problem with forgiveness before my husband died. However, afterward, because of considerable grief and suffering, I expected those around me to be especially sensitive. To be caring and loving and kind. But this doesn't happen in a lot of cases. You would be surprised at the things that come out of people's mouths. I couldn't wrap my head around the fact that here I was at the lowest point in my life, already at the edge of a precipice, and people wanted to further bury me alive. It felt like a stab in a heart that was already broken and bleeding. Forgiveness is a critical piece to overcoming the pain and moving on. It is more difficult when it is related to tragedy and loss, but that requires us to dig even deeper. Finally, I can say honestly that there can be no spiritual self-renewal without forgiveness.

PRACTICE JOURNALING

Journaling can be an excellent tool for spiritual self-renewal. In an interview, Michael Alcée, a clinical psychologist in New York, shared this with me:

> Journaling gives us free rein with our deepest thoughts and feelings . . . [It] is essential to our psychological well-being because it enables us to have a consistent, benevolent witness, one

> that we can bring along with us wherever we go. It is like having a portable therapist there to be a sounding board and guide through the often foggy experiences that our everyday lives comprise. Journaling allows us to access our right-brain-dominant feeling and associative side in the container of a left brain–driven, language-based task. It provides an important form needed to both contain and expand our deepest hopes.

As Robert Frost said, "I write to find out what I didn't know I knew."

Keeping a journal of our thoughts, experiences, insights, and lessons also helps with mental clarity, exactness, and context. It teaches us to express ourselves on a deeper level and to express our feelings.

So, I say start documenting your life with a journal. Document not only the sad times but also the happy times. Document the times that made you laugh hysterically, too. Write about the Easters and Christmases and holidays you have had—all the details. Write about the time when you asked your brother to be a groomsman in your wedding and he said no because he would have to help the bridesmaids behind the scenes, and his worry was that their false breasts might drop out. Write about that time your drunk aunt Betty threw up in your blind cousin Pete's lap. Write about the time when you were in high school and the girls would walk around in multicolored Velcro rollers at lunchtime (you know, the big, colorful, ugly rollers) so they would have perfectly coiffed hair after school to meet their boyfriends. Two out of three of those stories above were actual things that happened around me. (I bet you can't tell which ones they were!)

For Sue Matthews, president of the Taylor Matthews Foundation in New York and author of *Paint Your Hair Blue: A Celebration of Life with Hope for Tomorrow in the Face of Pediatric Cancer*, her journal was the inspiration for the book, which was published in June 2018. Her daughter, Taylor, was diagnosed with cancer at eleven years old and lost her battle at sixteen years old. Sue told me about her journaling:

> In the beginning, I wrote to her every day, which helped me stay connected to her. Then, I journaled about her life and illness, which also kept her alive for me and in touch with her. It was a great way to express my feelings by myself, in my own space, as well as a great release for me. It helped a great deal with my depression.
>
> While I was journaling/writing the book, it sparked memories of her that I had not remembered and gave me the ability to remember the good times. I am so fortunate that writing about her connects me to her and has now helped many other people. I have reread pages I wrote in the beginning (2008) and read what I write now. It shows me how far I have come.

Journaling is also great for more serious dilemmas. You know, the ones the biggest thinkers in the history of mankind were trying to solve. Many great intuitive thinkers like Albert Einstein and Steve Jobs wrote down ideas and could illustrate visual solutions to problems in the mind's eye. Isaac Newton had a "Waste Book," where he stored important passages from the texts he read. It inspired many of his discoveries.

20

RECIPES MADE FROM SCRATCH

The first wealth is health.

—Ralph Waldo Emerson

Healthy meals and proper nutrition are part of the tool kit necessary to master the art of recovery from disruption. After my husband died, I lost forty pounds in two weeks. I lost my appetite, and I couldn't eat. Nothing tasted good. My relationship with food had turned complicated, and trying to regain my appetite was as futile as a monkey grasping at berries that are fenced off just beyond its reach.

Food is as elemental to us as the air we breathe and the soil beneath our feet. The thought of food shared at home, with the sound of laughter, conjures up loving memories. Thanksgiving, Christmas, and Easter have one common element that unites us—the preparation of delicious meals—the ham and the turkey baking in the oven, the scent of which is the first thing that greets us on those holidays.

Life and food are inextricably intertwined. There is a thin line between life and death—and food is the currency used to maintain life. When a spouse dies, we lose the person we eat with the most. Our relationship with food becomes strained and evokes memories of a happier time, which can often complicate grief. The result is weight loss that can sometimes lead to malnourishment.

This is often the reason why older widows die shortly after their husbands. They have lost the desire to cook healthy, nourishing meals. Instead, grief, like a parasite, robs its host of critical nutrients through starvation.

From the time we started dating to the time Garfield died, we shared fifteen Easters and Christmases together, and I had cooked thousands of meals. During my grief, going to the supermarket was like going to the cemetery—a constant reminder of what I had lost. I cried as I walked through the aisles. On one occasion in Costco, my friend grabbed the trolley from me as I wailed. It was not a good sight—and Costco is always full.

It was on my sabbatical that I started eating healthy again. This is the Law of Natural Harmony and Balance. I started eating like our ancestors did: I went back to the drawing board and cut out things like pizzas, burgers, and fries. On my sabbatical, I ate mostly farm to table for breakfast, lunch, and dinner. I came up with my own organic recipes. My late husband's illness was hypertension related, and I knew I had to start eating better and getting the kids to eat healthier. I ate mostly a DASH diet (Dietary Approaches to Stop Hypertension), which is organically a traditional Caribbean diet in its purest form and is loaded with anti-inflammatories and antioxidants necessary for overcoming grief and trauma and that help with stress and relaxation. The DASH diet emphasizes vegetables, fruits, low-fat dairy, fish and seafood, whole grains, poultry, and nuts.

I also gave up sugar for the most part. I didn't have the cravings that I had for sugar in Canada because eating in the tropics was already infused with so many natural ingredients. My appetite shifted from one of refined sugars to one of natural fruits and vegetables. Physical nourishment is key to holistic wealth. If our bodies are undernourished and weak, we risk getting illnesses and diseases and, at a minimum, lose the stamina and energy we need to achieve our goals. On sabbatical, I had access to fresh fruits and vegetables I could pick myself every day just on the confines of the property. Almost everything I ate, including avocados, mangoes, cherries, bananas, and coconuts, was sourced from within a few feet of my house. I ate a lot of red snapper *escovitch*. We had fish prepared with ginger and herbs and red peppers. I had my own tropical plant medicine cocktail, made of fresh pineapple juice, coconut milk, sugarcane juice, and a dose of mint leaves—perfect for a blend of tropical vibes and mindfulness.

Gradually, my digestive issues faded, and I started feeling healthier by eating more homemade, nourishing meals. I ate less junk food and started eating food grown in my own garden.

Jennifer Smith, founder of Joy, Energy, Nutrition and a registered dietitian, told me in an interview that someone going through any type of disruption or trauma likely "needs to feel more grounded and centered in their bodies. They need to feel safe and secure in their survival and be connected to their tribe/community." Smith described foods that can help with grounding and a sense of centeredness and security:

- Red foods: five to seven servings daily of red, plant-based foods (such as tomato, cherries, raspberries, red bell peppers, red teas, red apples, red kidney beans, red lentils, and so on). Specific nutrients found in various red foods that are beneficial are vitamin C (which helps to strengthen our immune system, decreases inflammation, and balances the production of cortisol), iron (which carries oxygen in our red blood cells), and lycopene (a powerful antioxidant with many potential health benefits, including strengthening our bones).

- Root vegetables: three to five servings of root vegetables per week (specifically beets, turnips, parsnips, taro, burdock, and rutabaga, which are the best sources). In addition, fiber feeds the good bacteria in our gut (where 80 percent of our immune system is located), so root vegetables can help strengthen our immune system.
- Proteins: an adequate protein for every meal and snack, alternating between animal and vegetable protein sources. Proteins give our body structure and help the proper functioning of our immune system and adrenal glands, both of which come under stress following trauma and grief. Proteins make us feel more grounded as they help keep our blood sugar levels stable. Make sure that animal proteins are high quality (organic, grass-fed meats; free-range poultry), because meat from conventionally raised animals can contribute to inflammation.
- Mineral-rich foods: dark-green leafy vegetables, nuts and seeds, and whole grains. Minerals help us connect with the earth to ground ourselves. They also help provide our bodies with structure, function, and stability. For example, calcium helps strengthen our bones.

- Immune-enhancing foods: dark-green leafy vegetables, berries, and sources of omega-3 fatty acids (fatty fish and fish oils, flaxseeds, chia seeds).

EATING FOR HOLISTIC HEALING

During COVID-19, I developed a Holistic Healing course, currently offered at the Institute on Holistic Wealth, that I co-authored with my mother, who suffered from childhood epilepsy and who has a PhD in counseling. It was a combination of holistic healing practices—including medicinal food and herbs, as well as prayer and spiritual wisdom—that contributed to her healing from the illness. During COVID-19, many people realized the benefits of mindful eating to target immune-boosting foods that support our immune system to fight illnesses, as well as lower stress and anxiety. Foods that help fight viruses, such as ginger, garlic, and turmeric, took center stage.

During the days of my sabbatical and while living through a global pandemic, I rediscovered my love for cooking, and now I truly realize how important healthy food is not only to our physical and mental well-being, but as a contributor to our stores of wealth in the form of pleasure and health, as well as for holistic healing. Visit the Institute on Holistic Wealth website for more information on the Holistic Healing course.

21

DAILY EXERCISE

> If we could give every individual the right amount of nourishment and exercise, not too little and not too much, we would have found the safest way to health.
>
> —*Hippocrates*

Exercise saved my life when I felt the numbness and physical pain of grief start to take root in my body. At thirty-one, I felt like an eighty-year-old woman, so feeble and weak that in a supermarket one day I couldn't pick up an orange to put in a grocery bag. It was a mixture of sheer confusion about what to do and a physical inability to execute a simple task. When she realized what was going on, my friend took the bag and put in the oranges for me. This was about a week after my husband died. Because of the sheer trauma and shock of his death, my body felt as though it was physically shutting down. In addition to having extreme insomnia at night, I also wasn't eating well (if at all). My body became like a dead log; I had extreme numbness, stiffness in my limbs, and my stomach was in knots.

Exercise is as vital to our bodies as water and air. Like Cheryl Strayed in *Wild,* during my sabbatical I hiked every day to deal with anxiety and grief. Studies show that part of the reason why exercise makes you feel better is because of its impact on your brain. It will increase blood flow to your brain, allowing it to almost immediately function better. If you've been in a grief-induced fog, exercise can usually help you to feel more focused, almost immediately.

A study by Princeton University researchers revealed that exercising stimulates the production of new neurons, including those that release the GABA neurotransmitter. GABA inhibits excessive neuronal firing, helping to induce a natural state of calm. The mood-boosting benefits of exercise occur immediately after a workout and continue in the long term.

After I started exercising, I felt stronger and better overall. I walked daily with the kids, and just small things, like taking them to the park, helped my mental health. It also improved my self-confidence. Walking helped with mental clarity because it was on solitary walks that I had time to think about how to plan a future for myself and actually move forward.

My husband was a marathon runner who loved running to a fault. He also went to the gym on a daily basis. He was as fit as a fiddle right up until the very end. So much so that the ladies in the funeral home who dressed him for the burial remarked how fit his body looked. They said it had been a long time since they'd seen someone come in looking so good. While it was a little awkward, their comments were a testament to how fit he was and how good he looked—even in death. So, there you go. Even in death, our physical appearance gets noticed. If you want your body to look good even in death, start exercising.

Apryl Jones, actress on *Love & Hip Hop: Hollywood*, spoke with me about exercise in her life. She said she was "inspired by having two kids, by wanting to be healthy and not let myself go just because I became a mom. I was inspired by my breakup [from Omarion of B2K]. And when I started to see small results, it inspired me to keep going!" Apryl states that physical fitness helped "my mental space. My diet. Drinking more water. Having the knowledge about my body and how to fuel it properly."

Osric Chau, Canadian actor and martial artist, best known for his role as Kevin Tran in the CW series *Supernatural* and Vogel in the BBC America series *Dirk Gently's Holistic Detective Agency*, told me in an interview that a personal trainer got him back on the fitness track after multiple acting gigs and time in the studio:

> I used to live a very active lifestyle as a martial artist working stunts on the side, but when I started to act, I stopped training myself. . . . Last year, I met Eric the Trainer [Eric Fleishman], and he completely changed my life around. Not only do I work out every day now, I also maintain an even cleaner and regimented diet. He's shown me the ropes, and he must have done some kind of voodoo magic, because he has me enjoying going to the gym again, something I haven't enjoyed doing since I was a full-time martial artist! . . . A good workout can set my mood for the rest of the day. It's only been a short time, but it has already changed my life drastically.

I also got the opportunity to interview Tia-Clair Toomey-Orr, the 2020 and 2021, now five-time "Fittest Woman on

Earth" and Commonwealth gold medalist and Australian Olympian in weightlifting. Tia-Clair made history in 2021 as she won the CrossFit Games for the fifth consecutive time. Tia-Clair says, "CrossFit has changed my life. Simply put, if I never found CrossFit, I would not have found Olympic weightlifting and would certainly not have represented my country in the Olympics and Commonwealth Games."

Tia-Clair goes on to state, "My love for CrossFit didn't come immediately. However, over time I started appreciating and enjoying CrossFit more, and in turn, it became my passion. But what keeps me inspired in CrossFit is the desire to constantly improve in every aspect of my fitness, from running faster, running longer, lifting heavier, increasing my gymnastics ability, and many more facets."

Lea Genders, personal trainer, running coach, and fitness blogger, demonstrates the lessons physical exercise can teach us. She says, "Through running, I learned to set and achieve goals. I learned what it means to work hard and push myself past my own perceived limits. I set out to change my body, but instead I changed my whole life. Running gave me the confidence to earn my fitness certifications and start my own coaching business. Running taught me to take everything one step at a time."

If you aren't yet in a fitness routine, consider ways you can incorporate one. Even small steps make a difference. Several fitness influencers whom I interviewed for this book, especially moms with young kids, indicated that they multitask their exercise, from squats in the kitchen to laps up the stairs, always trying to get in the minimum viable amount because every little bit counts when time is limited. As Apryl Jones does, use small results to keep going and as a motivating factor to do more exercises. Sometimes we need an accountability partner or personal trainer, as in the case of Osric Chau, to get the extra push we need. Seek out trainers who have a strong reputation and who deliver results.

And if you already exercise, keep it up, with the added knowledge that you are contributing to your holistic wealth bank account with every workout.

22

JOYFUL HOBBIES

To be happy in life, develop at least four hobbies: one to bring you money, one to keep you healthy, one to bring you joy, and one to bring you peace.

—*Stan Jacobs,* The Dusk and Dawn Master

During and after my sabbatical, I found joy and passions I didn't even remember I had. I hiked every day, and I walked on sandy beaches weekly. I had the gift of time, and I truly rediscovered what it means to live. I also rediscovered some old passions. I had forgotten them, just as you forget the names of people you were once familiar with.

Hobbies are critical to self-care and boosting mental health. During the COVID-19 pandemic, hobbies rose to prominence again after global shutdowns and stay-at-home orders were put into effect. Similar to the Great Depression in the 1930s, when people engaged in hobbies to pass the time and avoid boredom, during COVID-19 people picked up pastimes such as making music, origami, and bird-watching. The Mayo Clinic has now added hobbies on the list of self-care strategies to help you cope during the pandemic. Hobbies allow us to find our passions and purpose in life, and they keep us in a state of natural harmony and balance.

Hobbies and activities that you enjoy are also a great way to connect with friends. Hobbies give you a way to take your mind off the stressors of everyday life. They allow you to relax and seek pleasure in activities that aren't associated with work, chores, or other responsibilities. They can ignite your creativity and help you find what you're really passionate about.

When I was about thirteen years old, I inadvertently created a vision board of all the things I liked—and I did it on my bedroom wall. While other teenage girls pasted pictures of celebrity boy bands on their walls, I had magazine pictures of beauty products such as luscious lipsticks and shiny lip gloss in vibrant colors. I also put up pictures of perfumes, with glass bottles that could be pieces of art. I did have a picture of Michael J. Fox on my wall, surrounded by my lipsticks and perfumes, but you know, *Family Ties* and *Back to the Future* were a big deal back then.

Later in adulthood, after I bought my first home, I bought magazines with pictures of interior design ideas—*Architectural Digest, Florida Home Magazine, Elle Decor, Canadian House and Home.* To this day, interior design has remained my hobby, and when I went on sabbatical, I renovated and decorated our new space with colors that were calming and with decor items that created a cozy feel: white faux-fur rugs, white candles, white duvets, and metallics in the kitchen, with black glass cabinets and a gray and black metallic backsplash. I created my own Zen retreat. These hobbies not only got me through some rough times, but they also brought me happiness and joy. I was surrounded by beauty inside and out, and it got me through the transition period. During COVID-19, I started the *Holistic Wealth Podcast with Keisha Blair* as a "pandemic hobby." To date, I have interviewed more than 150 amazing trailblazers, entrepreneurs, CEOs, influencers, and celebrities—strengthening my relationships as well as my resilience muscles. The podcast and the Institute on Holistic Wealth gave me the opportunity to help others achieve holistic wealth during a particularly traumatic event.

In times of disruption, people need an anchor to familiarity—something that they associate with joy, happiness, and stability. But more than that, our hobbies can be gateways to a meaningful career change. During COVID-19, with rising unemployment, people have been monetizing their hobbies on online platforms for additional income.

Jessica Meyrowitz turned her knitting hobby into a full-fledged company. Meyrowitz is the founder of knitting company It's a . . . Yummy, which makes handmade products from 100 percent merino wool yarn. Her DIY Mini Scarf Kit was featured on the *Today Show* as a must-have holiday gift.

Jessica states, "Knitting is perfect for the person who wants to bring more mindfulness and creativity to their life. Knitting is mindful, meditative, interactive, wellness-focused, and a great way to calm a 'monkey mind,' as well as keep your hands busy—which means less snacking. There's the mindfulness aspect, where I bring people in and we talk about being aware of your surroundings and touching the yarn, and taking cleansing breaths, and getting ready to do a practice that is mindful." Jessica turned her hobby into a lucrative business and created an opportunity for holistic wealth.

A survey of two thousand people across the United States by Exodus Travels, summarized in an article on the *New York Post* website, revealed that "83 percent of very happy people report having hobbies, or at the very least passions for certain topics of interest such as being active, getting outdoors and traveling—as opposed to 53 percent of unhappy people."

The article about the study goes on to state that "those classifying themselves as 'very happy' were 43 percent more likely to seek out new experiences than those ranking themselves as 'generally happy,' and 90 percent more likely to embrace new experiences than those who felt they were unhappy."

23

PRAYERS AND MEDITATION

I want to know God's thoughts . . . the rest are details.

—*Albert Einstein*

I grew up as an only child, and for years I worried about my parents dying and leaving me alone as an orphan. I overcompensated for this by reaching places too early. In elementary school, I skipped grades and was always the youngest in the class. I was accepted into the University of Oxford in England at fifteen but didn't end up going—my parents said I was too young. When I started my undergrad, I did the same thing in university and graduated ahead of my class. When my dean wouldn't give in to my demands of declaring a double major, I pressed until he had to yield to me, and carried extra courses during the summer. I did the same thing for my master's degree at Carleton University in Ottawa. I finished a whole year ahead of my class and graduated with the students one year above me.

My mom would always say, "You're reaching places way too fast. Just slow down." But I couldn't. I had to reach "somewhere" just in case my parents died. If I became orphaned, at least I would be able to fend for myself. It was as if I was competing with time itself—with my own self-made time machine. I felt like there was an expiry date, one which I created. My quest for financial independence began after I entered the work world. I was driven not only to save and invest but also to make sure I would have enough "just in case." However, the universe has a way of slowing us down. It wasn't my parents who died. It was my young husband. This was a major slowdown. Now I had no choice.

The great Protestant reformer Martin Luther is quoted as saying, "I have so much to do today, I'll need to spend another hour on my knees." To him, prayer was not a mechanical duty but rather a source of power in releasing and multiplying his energies. It was on my sabbatical that I rediscovered meditation and had the time to meditate and pray without a lot of distractions. I created the time and the space to be able to do this in a way that was highly beneficial to the renewal of my mind and body. I spent three hours every day (twenty-one hours per week) in the very early mornings meditating and praying and tuning in to my intuition—it was like having a straight line to heaven. Every morning at around three o'clock I waited in expectancy for that straight line to open up. During COVID-19, prayers and meditation, including mindfulness, took on even more significance as we faced collective grief. It is said that the last time the world saw something as tragic and all-consuming as the COVID-19 pandemic was in World War II.

There are several ways to pause: physically, mentally, and emotionally. A pause can be created by a walk around the block, twenty minutes of meditation, exercising, immersing oneself in a hobby, or simply taking a high-quality coffee break. The important point is to create time and space to empty your mind and then reflect and filter issues.

It was on my unpaid sabbatical from work that I realized the power of pause. I simply learned to be present. To be present with my emotions and my innermost goals and desires. That grief and that long moment of pause turned out to be my most powerful moment of self-realization.

There are two fundamental truths about living life in a constant state of busyness.

#1: BUSYNESS AND STRESS ARE THE THIEVES OF INTUITION

I conducted an intuition experiment after my sabbatical ended to see if my intuition would be as sharp as it had been when I relegated my busyness to the back burner. To my surprise, when I re-busied myself and lived in a constant hurry after returning to work, my intuition seemed to vanish. I no longer heard that little voice—or maybe it was there, but I had no time to hear it. I couldn't wait in expectancy, as my life had returned to the mad rush of meeting deadlines, attending meetings, and fulfilling requests. So, I decided once again to take time off for about five weeks. Again, like clockwork, my intuition returned—not just any intuition, the type that guided me on what decisions to make from the moment I awoke. Paradoxically, I had achieved so much more when I took the time off than when I was busy and most "productive." Furthermore, the achievements were different. They were in line with my personal mission and values.

#2: BUSYNESS AND STRESS ROB US OF REALLY LIVING

Busyness creates a cycle of constantly putting off the things most important to us. Reconnecting with loved ones, friends, and family, for example; giving our kids the type of quality time they so desperately deserve; connecting with our kids' school to engage the teachers on how we can be more involved and proactive in our child's education. Putting things off is the biggest waste of life: it snatches away each day as it comes and denies us the present by promising the future.

THE COST OF MINDLESSNESS

Operating in a state of mindlessness robs us of our ability to create holistic wealth. It's almost impossible to master the art of recovery from disruption if you're operating in a state of mindlessness. COVID-19 showed us how each decision could mean life or death—from not wearing a mask in a crowded place to not washing hands properly—and operating in a state of mindlessness can greatly increase the risk of a bad move. Mindlessness narrows our choices and weds us to single-minded attitudes. Professor Ellen Langer at Harvard University, in her book *Mindfulness,* writes, "The consequences of mindlessness range from the trivial to the catastrophic. These include an inhibiting self-image, unintended cruelty, loss of control and stunted potential." According to Langer, "Mindlessness limits our self-control by preventing us from making intelligent choices. Advertisers effectively cater to mindlessness, encouraging us to spend money on products we don't need when we're not thinking about it."

William James claimed that "almost all of us use only the tiniest fraction of our true potential. Only under certain circumstances of constructive stress or in certain states—great love or religious ardor or the courage of battle—do we begin to tap into the richness and depth of our creative resources or the tremendous source of life energy and the giant that lies sleeping within us." Langer writes, "When our minds are set on doing one thing or on one way of doing things, mindlessly determined in the past, we blot out intuition and miss much of the present world around us. If Archimedes had had his mind on only taking a bath, he wouldn't have discovered the displacement of water. By keeping free of mindsets, even for a moment, we may be able to see clearly and deeply."

How do you renew during the day? Taking several short breaks each day is effective in reducing stress levels and doing so also gives us the opportunity to renew ourselves. Meditation and prayer are easy ways to tune out the world for a couple of seconds and get back in touch with our inner thoughts and desires. To recover from disruption, we must take the time to pause, reflect, and renew ourselves.

24

SETBACKS

Sweet are the uses of adversity
Which like the toad, ugly and venomous,
Wears yet a precious jewel in his head.

—*William Shakespeare,* As You Like It

On the night Martin Luther King Jr. was assassinated, Robert F. Kennedy gave a speech to an audience in Indiana, not only to impart the tragic news, but to instill a sense of calm purpose and to reinforce the sheer greatness of humanity's ability to look beyond tragedy to embrace love. Kennedy's favorite poet was Aeschylus, an ancient Greek tragedian, oft regarded as the father of tragedy. In that speech, on that fateful night, he quoted Aeschylus: "And even in our sleep, pain which cannot forget falls drop by drop upon the heart, until in our own despair, against our will, comes wisdom, the bittersweet fruit of adversity." Given the legacy of

Martin Luther King Jr., it's greatly significant that Kennedy quoted Aeschylus.

Tragedies and obstacles hold the keys to unlocking your true purpose in life. It's hard to see obstacles and tragedy as hidden gifts, but these gifts have the ability to teach wisdom and to transform lives. These types of "gifts" are not shiny objects wrapped neatly with a beautiful bow, but real-life lessons in becoming more resilient.

After my husband died, I realized there are hidden gifts in grief. My sharpened intuition was one of the best gifts that came out of my grief. Another was gratitude. I had to take stock of what I was grateful for in order to move forward. We wouldn't invite setbacks into our lives, but when they occur, they are gifts that can add to our resources holistically. Like the opening quote from this chapter states, "Sweet are the uses of adversity / Which like the toad, ugly and venomous, / Wears yet a precious jewel in his head." If we can snatch the jewel from the ugly toad's head, we can create holistic wealth. Adversity allows us to become better rounded, richer in experience, and to strengthen our inner resources. Resilience is a key factor in creating holistic wealth, and you can't develop your resilience muscles without knowing how to overcome adversity.

When I was a little girl, my mother, Dr. Bernice Williams, a woman with seven university degrees to her name and a will of steel, had me chant my own slogan. She had to overcome tremendous obstacles from being very ill at a young age and missing school for five long years, from age nine to fourteen. Every morning, she watched a sea of neatly starched kids in blue-and-white uniforms walk to school from her bedroom window. Her hands and nose pressed desperately to the glass, she watched until they disappeared into the distance. She ultimately became a university professor and an adviser to a prime minister. She told me whenever obstacles came my way I should chant my slogan. No matter how high the mountaintops seemed—or how deep the valleys got—I should chant, "I can, I will, and I must." That was the slogan. She would say to me, "Keisha, tell yourself, 'I can, I will, and I must.' When the valleys seem so deep you can't climb back up, chant your slogan." I'm now calling this "the recovery slogan"—and each of us should have one.

As a child, my mother had fainting spells more than six times per day. She couldn't go to school, so she taught herself in between her fainting spells, slipping in and out of consciousness. Her teacher would send home the schoolwork with her older brother. Her parents thought she would die. After she gave birth to me, her father told her he was worried that she would die soon, and I would be motherless. She ended up successful enough to build her parents a house. She is still my rock and helped me through the most difficult time of my life.

Write your own slogan in your personal mission statement and chant it. Chant it as if your life depended on it. Chant it as often as you need to hear it.

Bridgitte Jackson-Buckley, author of *The Gift of Crisis*, whom I also interviewed, outlines gifts she identified as a result of a financial crisis her family faced after making the decision for her to be a stay-at-home mom. When her husband suffered a near-fatal stroke, the family income was nonexistent. After asking friends for loans to get through the crisis, she had to reexamine herself and the decision to be a stay-at-home mom. She realized her decision was a result of "looking outside of myself for love and to release my fear of abandonment by clinging to a stay-at-home situation that we could not afford." The gifts of crisis she identified are as follows:

- Letting go of fear to *be* with change and the discomfort of change.
- The emergence of new possibilities as a result of the crisis.

- Being responsible for the energy, beliefs, and perspective I bring to all situations.
- Awareness of the self-sabotage, projection, and fear-based thinking I brought to many situations.
- Letting go of deep attachment to specific outcomes.
- The importance of conscious decision-making with clear intentions and integrity.
- Trusting the nonlinear path and process of life.

Obstacles come in many forms—there's loss of careers or the business that doesn't work out, the illness or accident that changes everything. There's loss of love: the broken relationships or marriages that can't be fixed. And sometimes there's loss of life itself.

There are two key elements to remember in achieving personal growth and success:

- You are one hundred percent responsible for your life.
- You can achieve immense joy, happiness, and abundance.

After my husband died, it seemed like the pain would never end. A very good friend, in Ottawa, came to visit me one day at home and brought a pile of books on grief and widowhood. As we sat on a garden bench on the front porch overlooking the garden of pink and white peonies that Garfield had planted, I stared out into space with the pile of books in my lap, looking at nothing in particular, as I had done many times in the weeks following his death. She then turned to me and said, "Right now you're not ready to get back on the bus with us yet. You will just wave to us as the bus passes by." The bus was a symbol for work, careers, the rat race, and all the worldly pursuits we engage in to push our lives ahead.

She then said, "One day you will be able to smile at us on the bus as it passes by," illustrating that I was slowly transitioning to be able to appreciate and understand their pursuits, those on the bus of life. "When you're ready, you will be able to get back on the bus with us again."

As we spoke that day, I couldn't see myself getting back on the "bus," or even smiling at it. But I can tell you today I'm back on that bus—and I'm in the driver's seat. Everything in life is temporary . . . nothing lasts forever.

Building our resilience muscles starts with the way we process the negative events in our lives. Mental toughness is a prerequisite for personal growth and success. It is a prerequisite for holistic wealth.

25

GRIT

Wise men ne'er sit and wail their loss, but
cheerily seek how to redress their harms.

—*William Shakespeare,* Henry VI

I used to have pity parties with dry bones. I'm not even kidding. Doubt and fear—we used to hang out together.

In the early weeks and months after my husband died (and before I enacted the Law of Spiritual Self-Renewal), throwing pity parties had become my specialty. I was the self-appointed pity party queen, especially if I had a bad day and allowed the toxic naysayers to get to me and plant seeds of doubt and fear about my future. There were times they did plant those seeds and I felt weak. If you wanted to throw a pity party, I would be the ultimate pity-party planner—and I had all the props to make your party memorable, too. I could break out my army of dry bones with confetti and party hats to make your party extra special. You'd think you were in an episode of

Coco, the Disney-Pixar animated film, where Miguel visits the land of the dead and sees a multitude of jubilant, sugar-skulled skeletons. Like Miguel in the movie, at times I felt like I had taken on a skeletal mirage, just hanging out with the dry bones.

The dry bones—the fear, anxiety, and worry—they love a good pity party. You'd think it was Halloween every day. My sister, AJ Williams, whom I also interviewed on the *Holistic Wealth* podcast, is owner of AJ Events in Boston and Nantucket, and is ranked as one of Boston's best event planners. She's raised over $64 million for charity and hosted more than two hundred nonprofit events; she's planned parties and fundraisers that include the biggest names in TV and film, including Vanessa Williams; Earth, Wind & Fire; Common; Queen Latifah; Danny Glover; Jennifer Hudson; and Wyclef Jean, among others. I think it's in our genes, this party-planning thing. So, you can imagine my magnificent pity parties.

I would break out into pity-party mode just by thinking of my younger self, the little girl with the pink flowery dress and Mary Jane shoes with the bow and tie. How she looked young and innocent with flowing ribbons. She had no idea what she would later face in early adulthood. My heart sank. I felt horrible for the little girl, as she danced and twirled in her flowery dress with an innocence and naivete that only young children possess. If only I could snatch her away to avoid her pain, I would. But I couldn't. These thoughts were enough to make my heart race. And then the sequence of my life events would start to unfold, and again my pity party would break out—with the dry bones wearing party hats.

One day, I realized I had to kick them to the curb, the pity parties and the dry bones. They belonged in the land of the dead. I was becoming too much like them; my bones felt like a dead log, calcified and brittle, and I felt like a skeleton of my former vibrant self. I had kids to raise and a life to live!

I eventually got rid of them for good. I don't throw pity parties anymore, and if I do feel myself kicking into pity-party mode, or when I feel myself thinking about the little girl, I know how to flip the script. When the hurdles and the roadblocks inevitably come your way, whether professionally or personally, throwing a pity party is a precious waste of energy. In his book *Hardwiring Happiness: The New Brain Science of Contentment, Calm, and Confidence*, Rick Hanson says we are hardwired to focus on the negative experiences rather than the positive ones. We can be happier, he says, if "we train our brains to revel in the positive."

HOW TO ABORT OPERATION PITY PARTY

When the negative thoughts come, know how to arrest them. Normally it starts with the same old *tired* script. It's the script of your unraveling, the moments leading up to the fallout and the pain associated with the loss, whatever that loss was. Then the pitiful thoughts start where you feel sorry for yourself. It's a cycle, and as you think more and more, the pain turns into anger and then frustration that saps your energy, keeps you in the past, and prevents you from planning your future. People get stuck here for decades and never leave this phase. Tell yourself you will not get stuck in pity-party mode. You have to change that dial. You have to live your dreams. You cannot afford NOT to.

SILENCING THE INNER CRITIC

Managing pitiful, critical, or negative self-talk is a key element in learning to overcome a cycle of self-pity. In order to get out of pity-party mode, you also have to silence the inner critic.

You see, it's more than just stopping the script, because even after you stop the script, your mind continues to wonder. It thinks about how you handled the situation—who did what, who didn't do what—then it dispenses a judgment or a verdict. You either succeeded or you failed. If your inner voice deems you a failure, then another cycle starts. Tell yourself you are done with these cycles and thoughts. You need your energy and mental clarity to continue building your life. You can't afford to get bogged down in these thoughts. You can't afford to walk the streets with an army of a million dry bones following you. You are not the fearless leader of an army of Egyptian mummies. Your ability to achieve holistic wealth depends on you kicking them to the curb!

HOW TO FLIP THE SCRIPT

Perception is everything. If you see things through the lens of the naysayers or through a victim perspective, then it's hard to get what you really want in life. If you believe the negative messages, that nothing will ever work out or that life is against you and that you'll never succeed, then it may become a self-fulfilling prophecy. Every single part of your life can be changed by a shift in perception. I started telling myself my grief was a gift. Not the tragedy itself (that was horrible!), but my exploration of grief. I realized there were hidden gifts if I looked deep beyond the surface. It allowed me to outline a vision and a mission for myself. I was able to tune in to my intuition more than any other time in my life. I wanted to share my experience and help make the world a better place.

Here's how you flip that script. Name your goals, shout them loud and clear, and then write them down. You need the courage and the wisdom of Master Oogway from *Kung Fu Panda*. Yes, I said that right. When I was writing this book,

Alexander read the first two parts and said he loved it! He said, "It makes you sound wise, just like Master Oogway from *Kung Fu Panda*." I asked him why Master Oogway was so wise, and he said that he always has a vision for the future. Then Alexander looked at me with eyes wide open and his mouth agape as if in awe of Master Oogway and said the cartoon master once said, "There is a saying. Yesterday is history, tomorrow is a mystery, but today is a gift. That's why it is called the present." So, get out a piece of paper and write down those goals. Yes, claim your goals like they have your name written all over them. Today is indeed a gift; it is not the past. It is the present.

When we flip the script, we are eliminating the pity parties—the victim mentality. We are clearing out the negative messages of the toxic naysayers, and we are channeling a future filled with goals that have been met and superseded. We've cleared out the dry bones, and we're now removing the pity parties. Those pity parties give those negative emotions power, they fester and grow and become more powerful over time until we've almost trained our brains to start producing "pity neurons."

Nobody—not the toxic naysayers, not your boss, not your mother-in-law, pastor, mama, or the trees or the birds—gets to tell you how big your dreams should be. Your life will not be defined by one moment, and you are still writing that script. Nothing is ever easy or straightforward. It takes grit to stop the pity parties and move forward in the face of a terrible setback. The principles of holistic wealth are what got me through the tragedy of my husband's death. Every. Single. One. Of. Them.

My script wasn't finished when Garfield died. Even though I thought it was quite literally the end for me, it wasn't. The best was yet to come, both professionally and personally. I can say with certainty to you that your best days are ahead of you, if you claim it and go for your goals and never give up. The best is yet to come.

To flip the script, tell yourself: *I can, I will, and I must.* Tell yourself that you are not only a detour slayer but you are a conqueror and a road warrior. Whatever roadblocks come your way, tell yourself you have the grit and the tenacity to power past them. You will not be defined by dry bones, you will not be the leader of an army of Egyptian mummies, and you will not start engineering pity neurons in your brain.

26

DIGNITY

> Let none presume to wear an undeserved dignity.
>
> —*William Shakespeare,* The Merchant of Venice, *act 2, scene 9*

Going back to work soon after my husband's death was extremely difficult. As I opened my inbox, I saw old emails from my husband; we emailed each other every day at work. Facing these messages at work was a reminder of the loss, a reminder that my daily companion was gone. I felt like a stranger in a different land upon my return. People didn't know what to say to me. Making eye contact was hard for others. I was the manager of a team, and I had to keep my composure. It took every ounce of courage not to break down at work. I had to find a way to not only manage my emotions but deal with the questions from many coworkers, some of whom were seeing me for the first time since my husband's death. I was also now a single mom of two kids, returning from my maternity leave widowed—and my family dynamic had changed. Going back to the office after any disruption can be very difficult if there aren't any supports in place. Thoughtful "returnship" programs in the workplace are at the heart of what's needed after a return to work. This is the situation that millions of workers will find themselves in when returning to the office after COVID-19.

I worked on a case study for the *Harvard Business Review* regarding this very thing. It's always better in a professional situation to also consider your needs first and foremost, as well as the environment you're in. If you need extra time to deal with a divorce, care for a loved one, or recover from a personal illness, or are returning from a period of maternity leave—it's always best to communicate your needs. If the crisis is a result of something that happened on the job itself, then it's best to act calmly and rationally.

Professor Thomas Jay Oord, whom I interviewed for this book, is a twelve-time faculty award–winning professor who has written or edited more than twenty books and knows all too well how to handle a personal crisis at work with dignity. In the spring of 2015, he was laid off from his job as a tenured theologian at Northwest Nazarene University, in what became a national news story. The reason cited by the administration was declining enrollments in the theology program, but it was widely held that it was really because of his views on evolution. I had the chance to interview him, and he emphasized two major points about handling a situation like this: he did not retaliate or seek revenge. In fact, he talks about what forgiveness looks like and what it does not. In particular, he suggests that "an eye for an eye and tooth for tooth in the face of injustice is wrong."

Maria Leonard Olsen, a Washington, DC–based civil litigation attorney and author of *50 After 50: Reframing the Next*

Chapter of Your Life, states that "as an attorney, I try not to discuss my personal life at work, and to conduct myself as a professional at all times. What may be the talk around the office cooler one week will undoubtedly change the next week. When I got divorced, I vowed never to speak poorly of my ex-husband. It would help no one for me to do so. Anger is like drinking poison and hoping the object of one's anger is harmed. It harms the person who carries it, so I do not indulge in it. I pray for grace to live with dignity."

Amy Gallo is a contributing editor at the *Harvard Business Review* and author of the *HBR Guide to Dealing with Conflict*. She notes some of the core principles for handling difficult situations in her article where the case study I coauthored appeared, titled "What to Do When a Personal Crisis Is Hurting Your Professional Life," published in the *Harvard Business Review*. This is also a wonderful resource for returning to the office after COVID-19 and making adjustments or advocating for what you need in terms of building your resilience and bravery muscles.

Do:

- Determine what type of support you need—at home and at work (make a list).
- Tell your colleagues what's happening so that they feel compassion for your situation.
- Make clear, specific requests of your coworkers and boss so that they know how they can help you.

Don't:

- Feel you have to tell everyone directly—it's OK to ask close colleagues to explain to others what's going on.
- Share every detail of your situation; tell coworkers only the details that are pertinent to them.
- Assume that it will be painful to continue working during this time—sometimes going to the office can be a comfort.

THOUGHTFUL "RETURNSHIP" PROGRAMS AFTER DISRUPTION

After periods of any disruption in our personal lives, or in organizations, there need to be thoughtful returnship programs designed to help employees with the transition. As I stated above, after I returned to work widowed, after my maternity leave, I felt like I was in a new land. My life had shifted 180 degrees, my priorities and outlook had changed, I was already on a path toward holistic wealth and living a life of purpose and meaning, and the workplace seemed fairly static. After significant disruption, our whole outlook tends to shift—because there's post-traumatic growth. What surprised me most about my reintegration was the lack of awareness around how to deal with reintegration. At that point, I had already experienced near-death from childbirth at age twenty-seven (like many Black women, I am a maternal near-death survivor), and I had now experienced the death of my husband at age thirty-one. Around the globe, millions of people will be returning to work at some point in the future after the pandemic—the greatest such disruption in more than a century. Dignity needs to be at the heart of returnship programs—which should be thoughtful and responsive to the needs of employees. This is not just about instituting childcare and equal pay. It's about restoring and increasing dignity by ensuring that employees find meaning in their work and have proper self-care and wellness supports available. The Institute on Holistic Wealth has been coaching individuals to chart a path forward after disruption. Leadership is critical to ensuring the work environment enables adequate recovery. We are now living through a global work transition.

Dignity in professional settings is a great resource during times of disruption and crisis because it allows you to establish the parameters for how others treat you, protects you from naysayers and gossipers, and creates a container for emotions that may otherwise overwhelm you. Handling stressful situations with dignity is key to professional advancement and success, and it's also good for your self-confidence. When you can deal with stressful situations and maintain dignity in the face of a crisis, it is a key enabler of holistic wealth. In the end, you will earn the respect of your peers, colleagues, and superiors when you can demonstrate dignity, courage, and self-confidence.

27

INTUITION

> The intuitive mind is a sacred gift and the rational mind is a faithful servant. We have created a society that honors the servant and has forgotten the gift.
>
> —*Albert Einstein*

"It is by logic that we prove. It is by intuition that we discover," said the mathematician Henri Poincaré. In dealing with the world rationally, we hold it constant, and we become rigid in the way we operate because the rational mind is a faithful servant to doing things the same way. It is a faithful servant on autopilot. Through intuition, we grasp the flow of change and dynamism present in the universe. We therefore discover, and intuition becomes a catalyst for holistic wealth. Intuition is our inner wisdom, that little voice that speaks to us. It is the quiet voice that is hard to hear if you're not used to listening—it speaks through dreams, or spontaneously as hunches or gut feelings, strong urges, physical sensations, or memories.

While I was on sabbatical, I started tuning in to my intuition. It helped me overcome my grief. I had a feeling of being "tapped in." It was as if my intuition was in overdrive. I became hypercreative. I started to pursue and do things I had only dreamed of doing as a child. These were my childhood passions that I didn't get to explore after university, as I was on a straight professional path that allowed no time for creative pursuits. As a child and a teenager, my first loves were theatre, dance, and writing. I grew up doing speech and drama and won national awards for speech every year. I ended up being valedictorian at my elementary school because of those many awards in speech and drama. After university, I pretty much forgot how much I loved the creative arts. It was as if a piece of me had died, and I had wrapped up my past passions in a box and cast it out at sea. It was my brother, Donald, who encouraged me to go on a sabbatical and do the things I've always wanted to do.

On sabbatical, I hosted a national television show (the man I would end up marrying asked me to host it). At first, I thought he was crazy and out of his mind for asking me to host. Then I started interviewing many creative artists on television who told stories of overcoming setbacks and stories of how spiritual self-renewal led them to their passions and purpose, and it became far more meaningful. We also raised funds, through sponsorships, so one young musician could have the ability to produce music in New York City at a recording studio. Together with several partners, we were able to raise over $1 million (USD) in studio time and record distribution in New York for one young creative artist. These skills I had used in fundraising for charity and hosting a show were ones that had lain dormant, and it was only away from my regular day-to-day tasks that I realized I still had them and enjoyed the type of meaningful creativity they afforded me.

I also had the opportunity while on sabbatical to meet some amazing women and men who inspired me. These were people who had pursued their passions in the arts and had excelled at it, like Jasmine Dotiwala, British broadcaster and TV producer and former head of youth media at Media Trust; and Sharon Weiler, TV producer and broadcaster. These women were living their purpose and were wildly successful at it. I realized we can all embrace our passions and incorporate them in our daily lives. It can be a separate path, but it can also serve to enrich our current lives. However, there must be a deliberate attempt to ignite them, because they could be the fire that you need to discover your purpose in life.

I later realized that if I followed my intuition, I would start to make better decisions and have better results overall. Most of the best decisions I made in life came from listening to my intuition.

I interviewed Dr. Gail Saltz, associate professor of psychiatry at Weill Cornell Medicine and the author of *The Power of Different: The Link Between Disorder and Genius.* Dr. Saltz states, "Intuition is based on unconscious information amassed over your lifetime through experiences, memories, empathy, emotional reactions of the past. It happens quickly, often before conscious and more rationally based cognitive thinking has gone on. Therefore, one's intuition is often very spot on in terms of making good decisions for ourselves in all aspects of life, but unfortunately, often enough people are unaware of or squash their intuition and make choices based solely on conscious rational, data-driven thinking. Being aware of your intuition and allowing yourself to consider it in making choices, in reacting to situations, and in being creative can result in better outcomes that feel truer and are more satisfying in the long run."

Dr. Saltz goes on, saying, "Intuition can lead to more success in relationships and in work. That inner voice often taps into empathy, and the ability to react more empathically to others in your life and in the room often leads to more success in relationships of all kinds. But listening to your gut at work can also help you make more innovative and creative choices that can cause you to stand out and move forward with great success.

"Listening to your gut takes practice. Find quiet time to reflect on what matters to you most when considering a decision; which way do you emotionally lean? I say lean because intuition is not a highly emotionally charged decision from fear or high anxiety, it is a more low-key emotional decision from a place of this feels right or wrong, this feels expansive and true for me. Practice taking note of your immediate and initial reaction, before you move on from it. Go back and reflect on that initial reaction. Weigh it against other later thoughts based on pros and cons that you have thought out. Pay attention to daydream-like thoughts about the decision, a place intuition can pop up, too."

HOW CAN WE GET TO THAT STATE OF CONSCIOUSNESS? IT IS THROUGH INTUITION.

Intuition can lead us to live a purpose-filled life, and the grief that was suffered is almost always a catalyst for finding that purpose. It also leads to momentum and a laser-like focus.

Here are some pointers for using your intuition to live your best life ever—even after grief and tragedy.

CLEAR NEGATIVE EMOTIONS AND ENERGY

Clearing the clutter and waiting for that "line" to open up to hear those messages is absolutely critical. By "clutter," I mean all the worry and the grief, the chores to be done, the thinking about mundane things that fill our existence on a daily basis. It really takes meditation and a state of expectancy to hear that voice of intuition. It's channeling our desires and trying to find that healing so we can be on the road to recovery. That intuition can lead you to greatness. It is said that your body will tell you when you are operating in a state that you shouldn't be in. You feel agitated, anxious. Listening to that intuition can be the key to unlocking true potential.

Negative energy abounds during tragedy and grief. It's all around you somehow. There is self-doubt—what you "should have or could have done to prevent it."

There is also a lot of self-pity: "Why is this happening to me?"

Grief and tragedy become the perfect case study on how to rid yourself of these emotions that are there in abundance, through no fault of your own. But is this even possible? Remember that hobby you loved but never pursued? What are some of the things you always wanted to try but never got a chance to? Your intuition can lead you to live the life you've always wanted—even after grief and separation.

HARNESS YOUR INTUITION

Newton and Einstein had one thing in common: They mastered the art of harnessing their intuition to achieve missions that would change the trajectory of humanity. They took deliberate steps to answer the grand challenges of their time.

However, in order to become a game changer, it is necessary to harness the power of the intuitive mind. In one survey, seventy-two of eighty-three Nobel Laureates in science and medicine implicated intuition in their success.

Here are two ways to harness your intuition.

#1: SEEK SOLITUDE

The greatest hindrance in accessing your intuition is stress. People under significant stress use just a fraction of their mental and emotional capabilities. Activating your intuition requires, at a minimum, long periods of solitude. It comes with deep soul-searching and spiritual reflection.

#2: LISTEN TO YOUR HEART'S DESIRES

In chapter 19, I spoke about spiritual self-renewal and the importance of setting the direction of progress by embracing a mission and vision for your life. However, this isn't just about attaining position, fame, and power. These goals should embody service to humanity and making the world a better place.

I also had the chance to interview Dr. Susan Shumsky, award-winning author of fourteen self-help books, including *Awaken Your Divine Intuition*, *Awaken Your Third Eye*, and *Divine Revelation*. In the interview, Dr. Shumsky stated, "You are in touch with the 'still, small voice' of intuition; that inner voice will guide you to fulfill your heart's desires and live your true purpose and destiny. That inner voice is real and always guides you in the right direction. It's a lighthouse on your pathway that leads you to happiness and success. That inner voice is the true voice of your own higher self, which never fails and always speaks the truth."

If you listen to, test, trust, and follow that inner voice, you will make wise decisions with peaceful confidence. You will know what to do and what direction to take in every given situation. You will experience great joy, fulfillment, contentment, and peace of mind, because you know you are on the right path doing what is best for you.

In her book *Awaken Your Divine Intuition,* Shumsky provides a field-proven, ten-test system whereby you can test the authenticity of the inner voice and discover whether you are in contact with the true voice of intuition, or your ego, or wishful thinking. "It is essential to test the messages you receive, because they can be coming from the spiritual plane, the astral plane, the mental plane, or environmental influences. I recommend you receive your intuition only from the spiritual plane. Become spiritually street-smart and practice 'safe spirituality.'" Susan goes on to state, "People can recognize the spiritual plane because it is a state of wholeness and oneness, and an experience of perfect peace, perfect contentment, pure love, pure bliss, unbounded awareness, deep relaxation, and absolute fulfillment. If they are not having the aforementioned experiences, they are not in the spiritual plane."

DORMANT AND ACTIVE INTUITION

I noticed that my intuition erupted while on sabbatical, and prior to that, like a volcano, it stayed dormant. I often wondered what it was about soul-searching that caused intuition to come alive. I discussed this in an interview with Anji Hallewell, a self-mastery and performance expert from Natural Genius Academy.

With regards to dormant intuition, Anji stated that

it goes dormant from all the layers of conditioning that we go through on our way to adulthood. What we are told to do, not to do, which forms our views on how life needs to be. The more it becomes buried, the less awareness we have of it until eventually we forget we even have it. School is great at teaching children how to learn and acquire knowledge, but isn't known for teaching children how to stay connected to their true selves. The more we learn to rely on our rational mind, the more disconnected we become to our true inner voice.

There are a few things that you can do to re-ignite your intuitive side. Firstly, become aware of your inner dialogue. The voice in your head that sounds like you is driven by different things. This was beautifully demonstrated by Disney-Pixar's *Inside Out*, with the different emotions that could take over at any time. Mindfulness, meditation, and yoga are all great ways to gain this awareness.

The second thing you can do is to become more curious. Children are great at this; they are pure creative little spirits who are into everything. Over time, this becomes less pronounced as life becomes less fun, with more serious matters to attend to.

And, finally, ground yourself. When I spend time in nature, I shed any ego or invisible protective layer. This allows the humbler side to emerge. It is in this humble state that our intuition will shine through. For some people, this may be when they are drawing, dancing, or climbing mountains. Whatever it

> is for you, spend time doing it, because it will ground you and energize your intuition.

Intuition is an important enabler of holistic wealth. When we fail to tune in to our intuitive selves, we fail to make deposits to our holistic wealth bank account. Intuition operates like compound interest in our bank accounts; when we listen to it and make decisions that enrich our lives, it's like reinvesting interest rather than withdrawing it. Our intuition is an unending resource that never becomes scarce. It also accumulates on previous periods of a holistic wealth deposit, because when you make smarter decisions in life, it compounds in all other areas. When you listen to your intuition and it sparks your creativity, that allows you to become energized to find your purpose. Your purpose cannot be manifested with dormant intuition—you have to reawaken active intuition to be in tune with your purpose. This is why active intuition is like an ignition: it generates that spark—the energy needed to channel holistic wealth.

BUILD YOUR PHYSICAL, SPIRITUAL, AND EMOTIONAL ASSET PORTFOLIO

In Part III, I shared nine life lessons geared toward building holistic wealth by developing your physical, spiritual, and emotional assets:

1. Spiritual Self-Renewal
2. Recipes Made from Scratch
3. Daily Exercise
4. Joyful Hobbies
5. Prayers and Meditation
6. Setbacks
7. Grit
8. Dignity
9. Intuition

Below are nine actions you can take to increase your holistic wealth for greater physical and spiritual health, a deeper connection to yourself, and greater resilience during setbacks. Some of the items on the list are simply questions for reflection. Know that looking inside and getting to know yourself better are the first steps of building a physical, spiritual, and emotional asset portfolio. Choose to do one, some, or all of the following:

1. Reflect on what spiritual self-renewal means to you. Write it down, and then think of three activities that embody spiritual self-renewal in your life.
2. How can you continue to incorporate, or add, healthy eating in your lifestyle? Reflect on additional lifestyle changes that would support this.
3. Incorporating daily exercise will increase holistic wealth. Think about three ways you can do this.
4. Write down some of your favorite hobbies. Think about the ones that have the potential to increase holistic wealth in your life.
5. Reflect on prayer and meditation. How can you incorporate this more?
6. Think of setbacks you have had in the past. Write down three ways you have overcome them.
7. Think about some ways you have developed grit.
8. Think about how you can foster a culture of dignity in your workplace or at home.
9. Try to tune in to your intuition. Take note of your surroundings and what circumstances are more favorable for you to access your intuition.

PART IV

GOODWILL AND STRONG RELATIONSHIPS

28

SERVICE TO OTHERS (OVER THE HIGHEST-PAID POSITION)

Everyone has a purpose in life . . . a unique gift or special talent to give to others. And when we blend this unique talent with service to others, we experience the ecstasy and exultation of our own spirit, which is the ultimate goal of all goals. When you work you are a flute through whose heart the whispering of the hours turns to music. And what is it to work with love? It is to weave the cloth with threads drawn from your heart, even as if your beloved were to wear that cloth.

—*Kahlil Gibran,* The Prophet

Chasing after the highest-paid position is pointless. Service to others is the highest calling. When we go after the highest-paid position as the be-all and end-all, we go against the Law of Purpose, and we might miss our true calling altogether. The Law of Purpose states that we are here to manifest a certain unique purpose with our unique talents—one that we alone can manifest here on planet Earth—and that should be our ultimate goal. When we align our unique talents to serve humanity and address unmet needs, that's when true wealth is created. This wealth that results from expressing your unique purpose is not temporary wealth but permanent wealth, because it is an expression of the incomparable you. Salary is temporal, it is transitory, and its increase depends on someone else conferring that "favor" upon you. This permanent wealth to which I am referring is a state of permanent bliss. You are your greatest asset, and your unique and singular purpose here on planet Earth has nothing to do with salary.

Chasing after the highest salary is like a deer running across a busy highway—it's a doomsday proposition. Remember the naysayers in chapter 2? They think that salary alone is the sole arbiter of all true possibilities in life, but they missed the mark altogether. They used the salary as a weapon to instill fear and feelings of inadequacy, and as a way to outline all of life's possibilities. That's why they kept saying, "It's one salary now." They think the summation of life's potentialities are wrapped up in the amount of the salary. In that way, they measure life's possibilities by "the coin," which is in contrast to Aristotle, who in the quote in the introduction to this book instead advises seeking after a "better notion of riches and of the art of getting wealth than the mere acquisition of the coin." Those of us who think the fastest way to holistic wealth is through chasing after the highest-paid position have it all wrong. Your salary alone isn't sufficient to create long-term wealth. Your salary might let you live comfortably, but it doesn't guarantee wealth.

According to a 2021 Charles Schwab survey, respondents indicated that Americans believe it takes an average of $1.9 million in personal net worth to be "wealthy," which is considerably lower than the $2.6 million respondents cited in the 2020 survey. Due to the COVID-19 pandemic, people have been redefining what wealth means to them. Survey respondents also lowered the bar for what was needed for financial happiness to $1.1 million in the 2021 survey versus $1.75 million in the 2020 survey.[28] Chasing after the highest-paid position usually results in "lifestyle creep"—a bigger house, more luxury items, and more debt. It doesn't necessarily result in the accumulation of wealth. The truth is, few people become wealthy just from earning a salary alone. Once the job and title are gone, a cycle of poverty and hopelessness ensues, as we saw with the millions of people plunged into debt during COVID-19.

Furthermore, none of the physical wealth accumulated is buried with you; these things are essentially transitory. Not the money, the house, the car, or the prestige. Your title at work does not go on your tombstone. When the nurses gave me my husband's personal effects in a white plastic bag that night in the hospital, it really dawned on me that all of this is temporary. The only thing that counts is the positive impact we make in other people's lives. That is our only true legacy. When material possessions fade away, get discolored, lose their shiny appeal, the one thing that endures forever is our legacy—holistic wealth. When we are driven by going after the highest-paid position over all other considerations, it can result in missing your passions and unique purpose altogether. Being driven just by attaining a certain salary and job title is primarily an act of ego. It can be a recipe for disaster and for unhappiness.

---

28. "Schwab Modern Wealth Survey Reveals Americans' Changing Priorities Around Spending, Saving and Mental Health," The Charles Schwab Corporation, https://www.aboutschwab.com/modern-wealth-survey-2021.

Abundance and a path to holistic wealth are achieved when we ask ourselves how we can help humanity and align the answer to that with our unique talents.

Throughout history, we've read about the rise and fall of great civilizations—and most of this wealth was temporary, especially when it was self-serving and driven by ego. "My grandfather lighted lamps of wealth everywhere," wrote Rabindranath Tagore, "[and] they went out with him. All that remained of that festival of wealth were the soot marks from the burnt lamps, ash, and a single quivering weak flame." Tagore, born in Calcutta, India, and the first Asian to win a Nobel Prize in Literature, was referring to things that were driven by ego and to lavish spending that led to financial ruin.

Physical wealth and money, fame and fortune: they eventually fade away. I am all for ambition and saving and investing to plan for life's many eventualities (as you have seen in the life lessons outlined in Part II). However, the pursuit of power and riches, no matter the cost, to feed the ego and as social proof that one's life has been meaningful and valuable, is destructive and counter to the growth and progress of humanity collectively. The Law of Abundance does not mean you grab all you can for yourself because resources are abundant (that's actually a scarcity mentality). The Law of Abundance also does not suggest that, like crabs in a barrel, we join a race to see who can reach the top the fastest in order to grab whatever spoils lie up there. It's as if we think there is some award or trophy for reaching the top first.

In his book *The Seven Spiritual Laws of Success,* Deepak Chopra states, "Discover your divinity, find your unique talent, serve humanity with it, and you can generate all the wealth that you want. When your creative expressions match the needs of your fellow humans, then wealth will spontaneously flow from the unmanifest into the manifest, from the realm of the spirit to the world of form."

The Law of Reciprocity illustrates how we can live a meaningful life through giving, rather than just focusing on selfish pursuits. The Law of Reciprocity states that we give, and we will receive. It multiplies back to us. In other words, it is in giving that we also receive abundance and wealth.

Soon after my husband died, his close friend called and said, "You just started the race, and now it's like you have one leg cut off." At the time, that sentiment felt exactly right, my situation felt like an amputation. But now, looking back, I can tell you, life isn't a race to the top. We get to the point we need to get to, in time, if we live a meaningful life.

Researchers at Harvard Business School interviewed 2,000 millionaires for a study published in December 2018, considered to be the first of its kind to focus solely on this level of wealth. Professor Michael Norton, who led the research, asked subjects—the wealthiest clients of an investment bank—to rank their happiness on a scale of one to ten. All of the respondents said they needed two or three times as much money to be truly content. Specifically, a quarter of millionaires worth $1.5 million said they'd need eleven times more money to be perfectly happy, while one quarter said they would need six times as much. Interestingly, this "did not differ by wealth," and the perceived need that more money equates to more happiness was expressed even by those with a net worth of more than $7.6 million.[29] It is clear that wealth doesn't bring happiness and that the more money you make, the more you think you need to be happy.

29. Peter Lloyd, "No Matter How Much Money You Have You Are NEVER Happy: Even Millionaires Say They Need to at Least Double Their Wealth to Be Truly Content, First Study of Its Kind Finds," DailyMail.com, December 6, 2018, https://www.dailymail.co.uk/sciencetech/article-6466731/Money-doesnt-buy-happiness-Millionaires-say-need-double-wealth-happy.html.

Why do so many people tie their self-worth to their net worth and job titles and chase after the highest-paid position? So many people end their lives on account of work and money. There is an overwhelming sense of failure and shame that often comes along with living a different life than the one we think we're "supposed to have." This is one of the biggest and most toxic money blocks, and a money mindset that is actually built on scarcity. It stems from a belief system that a certain salary, or your net worth, makes you better or worse than others. Inevitably, this belief system can lead to disaster: on any given day or with any life-altering setback, it could mean that you see yourself (or someone else) as a failure. In some families, and in certain cultures, more prominence is given to those who are successful, "success" being primarily tied to net worth and material possessions. In a family setting, where this belief system is passed down through generations, this is an example of an ancestral money block. As we saw during COVID-19—where entire industries, jobs, and positions were wiped out in a matter of months—this belief system actively hinders recovery from disruption. Your ability to bounce back suffers when you tie your identity to a title or salary or net worth.

Amy Morin, international bestselling author of *13 Things Mentally Strong People Don't Do* and another young widow with whom I've shared personal conversations, states that people who measure their self-worth by their net worth may never feel "valuable enough." And it's not just wealthy people who define themselves by the size of their bank accounts—many people live beyond their means in an attempt to feel "good enough." But going deep into debt to create a facade of wealth backfires in the end, because while goods and services have monetary value, they don't reflect your value as a human being.

According to Amy, "A career helps many people feel worthwhile. In fact, many people introduce themselves by saying what they do: 'I'm a computer programmer,' or 'I'm a lawyer.'

Their job isn't what they *do*—it's who they *are.* Their career reinforces to them that they're 'somebody.' But basing your self-worth on your job title is a big risk. An economic downturn, unexpected shift in the job market, or a major health problem can put an end to your career and lead to a major identity crisis."

Heather, a blogger who blogs at *Altitude Adjustment* and lived in San Francisco for years, stated in an interview:

> San Franciscans want to know where you work, what your job title is, how many stock options you've been granted in the off-chance that your company will be the next unicorn that goes public. We like to know titles because it lets us know what monetary value people bring to the community. But, even within those titles, the value someone brings is rarely captured. What I want from a community are people who give their time to make it one they want to live in. While that may mean different things to different people, we must recognize that contributions to a successful society are varied and they don't always involve a highfalutin title or even a paycheck.

FIND MEANING IN LIFE

Finding meaning in life is an integral concept to world-renowned psychologist Martin E. P. Seligman, author of the book *Flourish: A Visionary New Understanding of Happiness and Well-Being,* and he includes this concept in his shorthand for happiness, PERMA, which stands for Positive emotion, Engagement, Relationships, Meaning, and Achievement.

Seligman states that if we want to be "happy in the long term, we need to strive for the 'Meaningful Life,' in which we find a deep sense of fulfillment by employing our unique strengths for a purpose greater than ourselves." The Law of Reciprocity (give and take) and the Law of Abundance govern this life lesson and demonstrate how we can live a meaningful life.

TAKE CARE OF THOSE LESS FORTUNATE

Abraham Lincoln said, "To ease another's heartache is to forget one's own." When you're in a state of bliss, you tend to see happiness all around you, even in the mundane. However, when you're in deep pain and sorrow, you realize how much pain and sorrow there is. After my husband died, I heard so many stories about other young men who'd died suddenly, leaving behind young families. I realized that my own healing would come by first reaching inward and then reaching outward to help others. Reaching outward takes the focus off ourselves and puts it on others so we can heal through giving back.

Patricia Karen Gagic was bestowed the Canada's Most Powerful Women: Top 100 award by the Women's Executive Network (WXN). I interviewed Patricia on the *Holistic Wealth* podcast, and she emulates a good example of this principle, as well as the Law of Reciprocity (give and take). Patricia, along with Serena Bufalino, nurtured Help Heal Humanity (www.helphealhumanity.org), a not-for-profit charity based in Canada that supports education in Haiti and Cambodia and has programs to end hunger.

According to Feeding America, one in eight Americans struggles with hunger. In 2021, 42 million Americans were food insecure.

During the COVID-19 pandemic, their organization helped to feed thousands from Haiti, Hamilton, the greater Toronto area, Ontario, Chicago, and Spain. In that same time, we saw how important it is for children and youth across the world to be given the opportunity to learn skills in a holistic environment catering to the whole individual.

29

MENTORSHIP

If I have seen further it is by standing on the shoulders of giants.

—Isaac Newton

Mentorship is a critical enabler of holistic wealth because it enables us to achieve success in our daily lives. Mentorship is also part of the Law of Continuous Learning and the Law of Reciprocity. There are so many kids and young adults who may never live out their dreams. No matter how smart they are, some just don't have the right opportunities. Mentorship is one of the best ways we can give back to the community and to the world at large. This is why mentorship is part of a holistic view of wealth, because it is a critical enabler that acts like a crane on a construction site; without that crane, those buildings and skyscrapers being built couldn't reach the heights for which they are destined. Many of us in our careers or even in establishing a business have had these cranes in our lives, people who help us to reach greater heights. They set our dreams on a path to reach the skies. They are activators of holistic wealth.

Mentorship can be a game changer in people's lives. When I started Aspire-Canada, a nonprofit initiative to help young professionals and students in college, and reached out personally to some of the world's best and brightest leaders to become mentors, I wanted to give back to society. I thought about my two boys, who had just lost their father. They would now need male role models throughout life. I went to my pediatrician and asked him how I would raise two young boys alone, and he said, "Find male role models for them." The problem was that I didn't have any male family members in Ottawa where I lived. My closest uncle lived in Toronto, a four-hour drive away.

I also contacted the Big Brothers Big Sisters of Canada, a nonprofit organization that provides mentorship to Canada's youth. It's a fantastic organization, and I was happy to reach out concerning my two boys. My kids were still very young at the time, so I thought I would wait a few more years until they were old enough to really benefit from the experience. I believe that mentorship or sponsorship can bridge the gap between someone achieving their full potential in life and someone who doesn't. I believe it can be a powerful catalyst for social change.

Joi (Brown) Pitts, senior vice president of marketing and brand partnerships at Atlantic Records, whom I met while on sabbatical and later interviewed, told me that her two mentors, Ronnie Johnson and Julie Greenwald, were critical to her career. She told me Ronnie allowed her to be her authentic self at work, and he inspired her to be ambitious and to strive for the best for her career. Julie encouraged her to take measured risks with her ideas (part of holistic wealth) and to make them happen. Julie is now chairman and COO of Atlantic Records. Joi has also made mentorship her passion through establishing HU United, a grassroots organization of over 3,000 Black colleges and universities; working on community activism; and launching Culture Creators, a networking and mentorship organization.

MENTORSHIP AND YOUR CAREER

Your career is like an organism that develops and evolves daily; it has tentacles and cells that divide and grow each day and requires the sum of many parts to allow it to thrive. In short, your career needs a systems approach for its growth and development.

Nowadays, having one mentor just won't do. You need a "multi-mentor strategy" that will equip you with tools and resources to have at your fingertips. With the rise of social media and information on demand, the need for advice in a fast-paced world calls for practicality and interactions unburdened by having to set appointments to meet over coffee one month down the road. Make no mistake, physical interactions in a mentor-mentee relationship are very important, but when you need a quick response at a moment's notice to adequately craft a good cover letter or a quick response to a potential interview question, having many mentors in a virtual environment, similar to the one at Aspire-Canada, is indispensable.

Dr. Michael Alcée, a clinical psychologist in Tarrytown, New York, in an interview for this book, told me, "Like Yoda to Luke Skywalker, Rilke to his young poet, or the original Mentor from Homer's *The Odyssey*, mentors are crucial parts of our apprenticeship into life's most important creative ventures. They help us not only in our school and work lives but also in the development of our character, purpose, and passion. Put simply, they help us actualize and become the person we are meant to be. We aren't meant to do this process alone; we all need our guides, and we all benefit from becoming guides in turn to others. Mentorship is a mutual gift that refines and develops the apprentice's raw talents while simultaneously inspiring and expanding the mentor's joy and delight in deepening and sharing their craft."

Michael goes on to state that mentorship is a "joint and paradoxical creative venture where the teacher becomes student and student becomes teacher. At its best, it becomes difficult to track who is playing what role, and that becomes part of its true power! We often think of mentors and mentees as primarily a hierarchical relationship, of older, more experienced folks teaching the young, but the lines are often blurred." As Alcée states, mentor-mentee relationships can be a reciprocal, egalitarian relationship, especially in the context of holistic wealth.

LATERAL MENTORSHIP

In the interview, Dr. Alcée pointed to developmental psychologist Deborah Heiser, who coined the term "lateral mentors." These folks can be of similar age and experience, but "have something unique and important to share from their own discipline or subspecialty." In her TEDx Talk, Heiser notes that this has become very common and powerful in the tech world and is the wave of the future. Working in this collaborative way opens new angles and solutions to old problems and creates a truly interdependent process. Heiser has spearheaded a program called The Mentor Project to bring tech and STEM folks, as well as a host of mentors from other disciplines, into the schools to inspire a whole new generation of innovators. Everyone can find lateral mentors, even outside of the traditional career setting: for example, stay-at-home moms or dads can find lateral mentors to enrich their lives.

MENTORSHIP AS "PSYCHIC INCOME"

Mentoring fulfills and solidifies a crucial part of our growth and development. As Michael Alcée suggests, mentoring is a form of "psychic income" (i.e., the energy you get from helping others) for the mentor, opening whole new sources of energy for growth and expansion. In the interview, he told me about his beloved uncle, who coined the term "psychic income." "It keeps the mentor connected to what the Zen Buddhists call the 'beginner's mind' while also exercising their expert wisdom. In other words, mentoring nurtures and sustains the proper yin and yang balance for being a creative and fulfilled person."

In that sense, mentorship falls under the Law of Abundance as well as the Law of Natural Harmony and Balance. I've discussed the notion of psychic income with Michael in deeper detail, and he stated that "psychic income also benefits the mentor by deepening and expanding the relationship that the mentor has both to himself/herself and the mentee, creating an I-Thou experience (as the philosopher Martin Buber called it). It allows one to feel a kind of profound connection and communion that occurs when we transcend ourselves. It allows us to therefore transcend our ego and really come from a place of soul work." In this way, mentorship as psychic income contributes to holistic wealth by adding to our holistic wealth bank account. This psychic income from our mentorship contributes to our transformation.

REVERSE MENTORSHIP

In a world where technology changes at rapid speed, reverse mentorship has increased and serves as a catalyst for holistic wealth when we are introduced to more creative and flexible processes. As Dr. Alcée stated, "Mentors help us to take knowledge and talent, and harness and focus it into a flexible process for creative work. They teach us how to synthesize what is complex and to constantly return to the fundamentals to rediscover how they can be reconfigured. They provide us with the courage, confidence, and openness we need in order to face the anxieties of 'not knowing' and to see that as an opportunity rather than a liability."

Mary Potter Kenyon, whom I interviewed for this book, is the author of *Coupon Crazy: The Science, Savings, and Stories Behind America's Extreme Obsession* and *Refined by Fire: A Journey of Grief and Grace.* It was after her mother's death that she began taking her writing seriously, so grief became the impetus for her to succeed. "I'd inherited my mother's notebooks and a memory book where she'd written that one of her greatest desires was that her children would utilize their God-given talents. Both she and my husband encouraged me to write a book about couponing, and I worked on that manuscript in her empty house the winter after her death. When my husband died seventeen months later, I was determined to sell the book they'd both believed in. I signed a book contract seven months after David's death. I've worked with the same publishing company for my subsequent books."

WOMEN IN STEM AND MENTORSHIP

Technology is the way of the future, and I'm going to go out on a limb and state that mentorship in the workplace will be essential for increasing representation of women in STEM. Sarah Zurell, whom I interviewed for this book, is the chief branding officer, executive VP, and one of the cofounders of Pavemint, the LA-based shared parking app. As a woman in tech, Sarah says mentorship between professional women, in particular, is one of her great passions. "Being a mentor is the most important direct action that any person can take to help move the needle toward true female equity. By sharing your own experiences and expertise with the people trying to walk a similar path, you help build the bridge toward success for all."

Sarah went on to state the following:

> Even though women are making great professional strides, they still only make up 20 percent of staff at the senior vice president level and 20 percent of line roles that lead to the C-suite and make up only 4 percent of the CEOs at S&P 500 companies.[30] The quota mentality (often explicitly expressed by men in the workplace by phrases like "this is our female perspective") breeds an unhealthy strain of competitiveness, not just between men and women, but between women at the same company.[31]
>
> Because so many professional women occupied one of the few non-male high-level positions in their companies and spent ten, twenty, or thirty years working twice as hard as their male counterparts to get and keep their jobs, many of those women have internalized a dangerous message: any other woman in the workplace is a threat.

---

30. Rachel Thomas et al., *Women in the Workplace 2018*, study published by McKinsey & Company and Leanin.org, https://womenintheworkplace.com/#download-charts.
31. Bonnie Marcus, "The Dark Side of Female Rivalry in the Workplace and What to Do About It," *Forbes*, January 13, 2016, https://www.forbes.com/sites/bonniemarcus/2016/01/13/the-dark-side-of-female-rivalry-in-the-workplace-and-what-to-do-about-it/#7eeecfd65255.

> And what more *brilliant* way to keep smart, independent, and creative women from thriving, and from banding together in the workplace, than to tell us, subtly, and in so many different ways, *"There is only room for one"*?

BECOME A MENTOR

Kyle Elliott, member of the Forbes Coaches Council, states that "mentorship allows you to leave a legacy and further your impact. You are shaping the next generation by being a mentor."

Tim Toterhi, founder of Plotline Leadership and author of *The HR Guide to Getting and Crushing Your Dream Job*, has this to say about mentoring:

> The best of [mentors] shift seamlessly from teacher to coach, confidante to counselor, cheerleader to drill sergeant . . . They have the eye of an artist, the patience of a craftsman, and a curious disposition that enables them to be the architects of possibility . . . [W]hen you mentor others you build a community of those who are better for having known you. Your reputation as a talent developer grows and you are rarely at a loss for a new employee, teammate, or helping hand. That's how leaders are made. Of course, mentors also benefit by knowing their efforts spark duplication. If you had a good mentor, chances are you'll be one.

There are many places to seek out opportunities to become a mentor:

- **Your current organization.** Search within your current organization to become a mentor. Most organizations have developed mentorship programs, and you just need to step forward and identify yourself as a potential candidate.
- **Online opportunities.** There are mentorship initiatives similar to Aspire-Canada where you can reach out to the organization via email to let them know your background and why you would like to volunteer. These organizations are always looking for volunteers. There is less of a time commitment, and you can interact with as many people as you'd like.
- **Boards.** There are also opportunities to mentor others as part of a board. This also widens your network and allows you to find opportunities to sit on the board of an organization that directly aligns with your mission.

30

THE GIFT OF HELP

The universe operates through dynamic exchange . . . giving and receiving are different aspects of the flow of energy in the universe. And in our willingness to give that which we seek, we keep the abundance of the universe circulating in our lives. This frail vessel thou emptiest again and again, and fillest it ever with fresh life. This little flute of a reed thou hast carried over hills and dales, and hast breathed through it melodies eternally new . . . Thy infinite gifts come to me only on those very small hands of mine. Ages pass, and still thou pourest, and still there is room to fill.

—*Rabindranath Tagore,* Gitanjali

My husband was a big believer in community service and giving back. He had the "gift of help." Even when he had just started a new family, he found ways to help build his community and give back. Whether you are new to your community, city, or country, you can give back. The Law of Reciprocity states that when you give, you shall also receive. Giving back contributes to holistic wealth. In helping others, we create happiness both in the life of the receiver as well as in our own lives.

He helped Habitat for Humanity in Ottawa build houses for the poor on weekends when he was off work. He was also a certified general accountant and partnered with the Certified General Accountants Association, which helps the poor and elderly with filing their income tax returns during tax season. At times, he had a long lineup of seniors waiting for him to help them file their taxes free of charge. Later, as the financial controller at Boyden Canada, he partnered with his colleagues to participate in the "Rattle Me Bones" race in support of bone cancer research at the Ottawa Hospital. He was always looking for a way to give back. He even coached a team of young female soccer players in the community.

After I returned to Canada from my sabbatical, I realized I needed to be a positive influence and use whatever means I had to make a valid contribution to society. I wanted to help young widows, help young people in university, and most of all I wanted to write about it. That's when I started Aspire-Canada as well as the scholarship fund to give back. I truly believe that in each of us is the ability to have a lasting impact.

We hear, for instance, of countless wealthy pro athletes and sports stars losing their riches and wealth because of bad spending habits or being taken advantage of by bad managers. According to CNBC, "Sixty percent of NBA players go broke within five years of departing the league. And 78 percent of former NFL players experience financial distress two years after retirement."[32]

Alan Santana, whom I interviewed for this book, is a former professional Olympic boxing champion and author of *Unprotected: A Tactical Approach to Boxing, Business, and Life*, which was written to protect athletes as well as to educate them on the business side of the sport, including management and contracts. Alan states that "athletes lose millions of dollars because of bad money management and not realizing that their career will not go on forever, and in many cases by the time they realize it, the money is all gone. Overspending is a huge problem with many of these professional athletes. They overextend themselves by buying too many material things, be it homes, cars, or jewelry. Many athletes are taken advantage of by their managers."

Alan retired from professional boxing in 1990 after being involved in a career-ending traffic accident. He became very depressed after his boxing career ended, especially because it was not on his terms. He had to dig deep inside himself in order to figure out how he would pull himself out of a deep state of depression that he hid from his entire family, including his wife.

Alan found an outlet in writing and also in mentoring children in elementary schools in California. He founded No Teen Riders, a nonprofit that helps to educate teenage drivers across the country, as well as "Saving Lives One Teen Driver at a Time." He became an ambassador for the Read60 program, which teaches elementary school children to read at least sixty minutes a day. Alan believes that regardless of your background, you can overcome any obstacle that life may throw at

---

32. Chris Dudley, "Money Lessons Learned from Pro Athletes' Financial Fouls," CNBC online, May 14, 2018, https://www.cnbc.com/2018/05/14/money-lessons-learned-from-pro-athletes-financial-fouls.html.

you and do whatever you set out to do. At fifty-seven years of age, Alan figured out how to beat depression and give back to society by being a positive role model for teens and younger schoolchildren across the country.

Paying it forward is one of the best ways we can give back to society while increasing our own happiness. It not only improves our self-confidence but it releases feelings of satisfaction to be able to help someone else. It can also help others attain holistic wealth from learning from our own experiences. Alan Santana's example, as it relates to pro athletes, shows how even the wealthy need guidance on how to keep and protect their assets.

IN HELPING OTHERS, YOU HELP YOURSELF

This is the Law of Reciprocity at work. We see it with more-concrete actions (where the terms of mutual gain are explicitly laid out and negotiated up front), but when it is totally unexpected, it's always a moment in which you watch the laws of the universe unfold. Some of the leaders and best business minds that I reached out to in setting up Aspire-Canada have helped me grow both personally and professionally. When I sent out "cold" emails to each one of them separately, I didn't know that their lives would become a lesson to me in how to achieve greatness—how to leave a legacy and set the direction of progress in my life. There was no talk about monetary gain or publicity or otherwise—this was strictly about helping others through voluntary work. Many of them have gone on to achieve even greater things since I asked them to become mentors. Never underestimate the growth that can take place with individuals on a personal and professional basis, and how this can impact your life. You can set the direction of progress in your life and launch out to do something new—even if there isn't a monetary gain. For example, when I reached out to Michele Romanow to come on board as a mentor, she had just started a new online business in Toronto called Buytopia.ca. That was in 2014, and now Michele is one of the top female entrepreneurs in Canada. When I asked her to come on board she not only said yes, but she also said, "Let me know how I can help." Michele joined the cast of CBC's *Dragons' Den Canada* and was selected as a Young Global Leader by the World Economic Forum. Her life and progress as a young female in a male-dominated field (high-tech) has been a lesson to me.

Dave Kerpen, CEO of Likeable Local and *New York Times* bestselling author of *The Art of People: 11 Simple People Skills That Will Get You Everything You Want*, is also a great example. He was one of my earliest supporters, and his people skills are truly extraordinary. It's no wonder he is the #1 LinkedIn Influencer of all time—ahead of Bill Gates, Jack Welch, and Mark Cuban.

When I reached out to Dave to ask him about his own personal mentors, Dave told me about a short flight that changed his life. He was sitting in the front row of coach, and just before the flight took off, an older man got up from first class, which was crowded, and sat down in his row, just across the aisle.

As the plane took off, Dave peered to his right and saw the older man reading a paper and noticed the words on the page: "My dear friend, the late Ted Kennedy . . ."

Intrigued by what he saw, he read on, and saw the following words soon thereafter:

"When I wrote the new GI Bill . . ."

He then realized that he was sitting next to a congressman! Excited, but still not knowing who he was, he put out his hand and said, "Excuse me. Sorry to bother you, but I just wanted to say it's an honor to meet you. I'm Dave Kerpen."

"Great to meet you, Dave. I'm Senator Frank Lautenberg," he replied.

They proceeded to talk for the next forty-five minutes, the entire flight to Boston.

Senator Lautenberg gave Dave his business card, told him he really enjoyed meeting him. Dave thanked the senator profusely and told him he'd given him a lot to think about in terms of creating a legacy as he had done.

"One more thing, Dave," Senator Lautenberg said. "I want to show you a picture of my greatest legacy." Senator Lautenberg pulled his phone out of his pocket and proceeded to show Dave a picture with several people.

"These are my four kids and seven grandchildren, Dave. This is my greatest legacy."

As this story demonstrates, holistic wealth is about achieving wealth in all areas of your life. Many people achieve financial wealth at the expense of their families and personal relationships, but, as the story above illustrates, this doesn't have to be the case.

31

RELATIONSHIPS WITH THE RIGHT PEOPLE

People . . . who have a kind of undefined social power . . . make the world work by spreading ideas and information, and by connecting varied and isolated parts of society.

—Malcolm Gladwell, "Six Degrees of Lois Weisberg," New Yorker, *1999*

True luxury isn't material, it's about people. It's the privilege of connecting with others to experience something more precious: their way of looking at things and their unique perspective.

As Dave Kerpen mentioned in an interview, "Networking is awesomely powerful. The key difference, though, in the way most people network versus the way you should network is the best networkers look to figure how they can help the people in the room, and add the most value, *not* how the people in the room can help them."

In my executive leadership program at Harvard University, I learned about homogenous and heterogenous social ties. Homogenous (or strong ties) are normally people closest to us, like family members and friends; these people have the same networks as we do. Heterogenous ties (weak ties) are more diverse, have a far reach, and normally expose us to new ideas, innovation, and creativity. These weak ties can be powerful if we try to tap into them. In the chapter on mentorship, I spoke about having a whole ecosystem of mentors with different backgrounds and different areas of expertise. The ecosystem thesis here is the same—these weaker ties can be highly beneficial in achieving holistic wealth.

In 1999, *New York Times* bestselling author Malcolm Gladwell penned an article in the *New Yorker* titled "Six Degrees of Lois Weisberg." In it, he recounts the story of Lois Weisberg, Chicago's commissioner of cultural affairs. He describes how Weisberg "is connected, by a very short chain, to nearly everyone. In the course of her seventy-three years she has become acquainted with a wide variety of people from all different walks of life." The article explores whether "people like Lois—who have a kind of undefined social power—actually make the world work by spreading ideas and information, and by connecting varied and isolated parts of society." Even though Lois had no political power or economic power, she used her relationships to forge ahead with her activism and personal mission.

Stanley Milgram established the concept of six degrees of separation in the 1960s. In this experiment, Milgram found that "a very small number of people are linked to everyone else in a few steps, and the rest of us are linked to the world through those few."

In his classic book *Getting a Job: A Study of Contacts and Careers,* sociologist Mark Granovetter examined the importance of "weak ties" (or heterogenous ties). He found that most people obtained their jobs through acquaintances, not close friends—in effect through heterogenous ties. Granovetter emphasized the importance of knowing people who know many people, because then you're just one "chain length" away from a good opportunity.

Through my work on reaching out to influencers, leaders, and various mentors for Aspire-Canada, I've come up with a categorization when networking for professional or business purposes, based on the people you may meet and how they may influence your work. In its very essence, it's networking for holistic wealth.

HOLISTIC WEALTH CONNECTORS

Connectors are some of the most generous people you will ever meet because they will readily connect you with their network. Like Lois Weisberg, some of these superconnectors, who have expert knowledge in their field, operate like "anchor firms" in their communities or in superclusters in which they are linked. They act like satellites in their communities and make connections for mutual benefit to everyone in their network or cluster. This is how connectors can enable you to achieve holistic wealth—they act as "catapulters" to take your mission to the next level. In his bestselling book *The Tipping Point: How Little Things Can Make a Big Difference,* Malcolm Gladwell also explores how connectors can spread ideas to epidemic-like proportions because they "occupy many different worlds and subcultures."

One such connector I know is Gail Cayetano Classick, cofounder of The Heart Series conference in Los Angeles and partner in the Cayetano Legacy Collection. I met Gail while I was on sabbatical, and she showed me how connectors operate on a practical level to enrich the lives of others around them. Gail has a big heart and was always invested in everyone's success. Gail belongs to many different social networks. While most of us occupy three or four main social circles—including work, family, and perhaps one other club membership or church—people like Gail Cayetano Classick occupy many different far-reaching social circles with tremendous social or "soft" power. Gail has connected me with numerous remarkable individuals, including Sharon Weiler, founder and creator of the Miami-based Daily Flash TV. While on sabbatical, I collaborated with Sharon to do a TV giveaway for the young widows of US veterans. Another superconnector I know is Rachel Goldstein, founder of Rachel Paige Goldstein Consulting. When I asked Rachel to come on board as a mentor at Aspire-Canada, she not only said yes, she offered to hop on a call with me to see how I could get the initiative off the ground. She basically opened her Rolodex and offered to connect me with additional individuals who might be able to come on board as mentors. She also connected me to Louise Flory at Marie Forleo International to see how we could spread a positive message for women globally. Rachel is also an amazing person with a big heart, and her company, Agent of Change, has raised over $70 million to date for various initiatives related to women's rights, veterans' issues, peace, social justice, and the arts. Rachel was a strategic adviser and core organizer of the inaugural Women's March on Washington and is a senior adviser at the Milken Institute. Connectors are enablers of holistic wealth because they provide us with links to relationships that are critical to building careers or new endeavors. These loose ties that connectors facilitate are important to holistic wealth, as they increase our creativity by introducing us to new ideas and a diversity of thought.

HOLISTIC WEALTH CHEERLEADERS

Cheerleaders also have big hearts. They cheer on everyone in their circle, and they radiate positivity. They find some way to help out, and even if they break bad news to you, they are optimistic. One such cheerleader is Dave Kerpen. He ends his emails with his signature phrase "YOU rule!" Not only does it put a smile on your face, but it gives you confidence to go on. We need cheerleaders in our lives, whether we're starting a new initiative or just living our day-to-day professional lives. These cheerleaders give you a boost that increases your self-confidence to achieve holistic wealth. Without these cheerleaders in our lives, we get stuck in a phase where we feel we can't make it. Another such cheerleader in my life is my mom. She has cheered me on even in times when I felt I wouldn't make it, and this gave me the courage to keep striving, to keep being better.

HOLISTIC WEALTH INFLUENCERS

Celebrities and influencers don't always have to fall in the camp of "Hollywood's A-list." They can be well-known authors, revered professors, and other influencers you may know. You may come across one or more in your life, and the ones who have big hearts can propel you forward if you get the opportunity to interact with them. Loren Ridinger, SEVP of SHOP.COM, is an influencer and celebrity in her own right and someone who not only has a big heart but is always helping others. When I asked her to become a mentor, she was supportive and became a contributor to the platform immediately. In an interview with me on the *Holistic Wealth* podcast, Loren told the story of her struggles with starting her new company. At the time of launching the business, it was bringing in just $1,000 per month. Everyone told her she was crazy; hearing that, she decided to shut out the negative talk and naysayers, and keep believing. She knew eventually their day of success would come. Loren went on to state, "It wasn't about the products at first. It was about belief. Believing we could do it. Believing we could get the cream of the crop. Don't quit just because it's not happening on your clock. Progress takes time." On the podcast, Loren advised women to make goal-setting a priority: "If I make a project, I create goals. I do twenty-eight-day challenges to achieve goals. Hold yourself accountable and put some dates on paper. Be passionate and know your 'why.' If you know your why, then you will figure out your 'how.'" Loren Ridinger is now an Honorary Certified Holistic Wealth™ Consultant with the Keisha Blair Institute on Holistic Wealth.

I interviewed Suzanne Brown, founder of Mompowerment and a TEDx speaker, who had a few suggestions on developing these relationships. Such development is especially important after COVID-19, as many people are changing jobs, switching industries, or starting businesses. A critical part of the art of recovery from disruption is your networking plan (part of your Holistic Wealth Portfolio under your Relationships Asset portfolio subsection). During COVID-19, many millennials came to me for help and advice with changing their careers and revising their résumés to gain the attention of employers.

Suzanne's suggestions for developing these relationships include the following:

- **Understand what you're looking for and why.** For example, are you hoping to change jobs within your company, or are you looking for a new type of project in order to grow a skill set? These types of differences impact who you network with, how you position yourself, and what you ask for.

- **Make the effort to create a networking plan that includes your strategy and goals** (e.g., number of new people to meet each month and the kind of people you want to meet with, such as senior leaders). Hold yourself accountable to your goals. And reward yourself for hitting your goals in a meaningful way.
- **Take time to develop relationships.** You don't want to be looking for strategic relationships when you need them. You want to develop them over time and create a natural rapport.
- **Relationships are a two-way situation.** Consider what you can offer in a relationship, especially with a mentor or sponsor.
- **Prepare for each conversation.** Know what you want from each interaction so that you can have control of what you want to cover. Consider preparing an agenda, even if you don't share it. The idea is to make the most of each chat, since you'll likely not meet with the individual again for a while.

Dr. Dinorah Nieves, PhD, a.k.a. "Dr. D," coaching consultant on the Oprah Winfrey Network's *Iyanla: Fix My Life*, says "successful professional relationships require many of the same skills required by successful romantic relationships and healthy and lasting platonic friendships. The relationships must be rich."

R.I.C.H. is an acronym she came up with for some of the primary ingredients required of healthy and successful relationships:

- **Respect:** Mutual understanding and acknowledgment of the value that each person brings to the relationship and to the larger goals of the relationship.

- **Introspection:** Constant self-evaluation and growth that strengthens character and motivates healthy change.
- **Commitment:** Dedication to a shared vision of the relationship or to a purposeful contribution that the relationship makes to an important cause.
- **Honesty:** Transparent and consistent communication about what each person is feeling, needing, wanting, requesting, expecting, offering, and grateful for.

Another important ingredient of healthy and successful relationships (professional or otherwise) is trust, which is an offshoot of honesty.

32

A PLATFORM THAT REPRESENTS YOU

> When you discover your essential nature and know who you really are, in that knowing itself is the ability to fulfill any dream you have, because you are the eternal possibility, the immeasurable potential of all that was, is, and will be.
>
> —*Deepak Chopra,* The Seven Spiritual Laws of Success

So, let's say you have built your mission statement with your values and vision, and you realize that part of your purpose is to reach out to help others achieve a singular goal. Remember that holistic wealth occurs when you discover your passions and then align those passions with serving others by identifying and filling their unmet needs. In order to do this, or execute this task, you will have to build a platform that truly represents you. Build a platform that is truly representative of your brand. Don't focus too much on social media and the number of followers at first. That doesn't necessarily translate into impact. Your platform isn't your social media account. Many people can buy followers on Twitter, Facebook, and Instagram and call that a platform. It isn't one.

Your platform and public narrative is the summation of the things you've achieved, your struggles and setbacks, and the steps you've taken to overcome them. It's the big and little things that add flavor to your life. It's what has made you into who you are—it's the totality of you—and it represents moments when you convey your "story of self." Your platform is The Incomparable You. If we get the important things right, our brand and message and mission will all align. Our platform is a testament to our passions and desire to have an impact in whatever niche we've chosen and to align our mission with our unique talents. I have no doubt that tragedy and grief, female economic empowerment, and overcoming setbacks will impact my writing for years to come.

You are able to change your life and get the important things right. You need to tell yourself that you can do it. Your platform is your community, which is the group that the message starts to resonate with and then results almost in a movement.

Having a platform that represents you also means getting involved in causes you believe in that will advance humanity. When you do this, it reinforces your own brand and inspires others to join you.

OPRAH WINFREY

Oprah has built the greatest platform of all time. She is the summation of it, and everything she does and advocates for is wrapped up in her overall mission and purpose. In May

2018, Oprah addressed the students of the University of Southern California's Annenberg School for Communication and Journalism. Oprah focused on the importance of speaking out against hatred and deceit, appealing to graduates to get the important things right—a colossal task facing today's journalists. She appealed to the graduates to spread the truth and impart wisdom and justice through journalism, declaring, "You will become the new editorial gatekeepers, an ambitious army of truth seekers, who will arm yourselves with the intelligence, the insight, and the facts necessary to strike down deceit."

Speaking to the soon-to-be-journalists, Oprah reminded the graduates of the power they have to give voice to those who otherwise would be without one, encouraging them to use the platforms they have been given to "give voice to people who desperately now need to tell their stories."

She went on to say, "And this is what I do know for sure, because I've been doing it a long time: If you can just capture the humanity of the people of the stories you're telling, you then get that much closer to your own humanity. And you can confront your bias and you can build your credibility and hone your instincts and compound your compassion. You can use your gifts, that's what you're really here to do, to illuminate the darkness in our world."

Having a platform is a powerful thing. I see too many things wrong in today's world with misuse and abuse of platforms. Getting the important things right means advancing humanity instead of pushing selfish goals.

33

TIME SPENT WITH FAMILY, AND HOLIDAYS THAT COUNT

The voice of parents is the voice of gods,
for to their children they are heaven's
lieutenants.

—*William Shakespeare,* Double Falsehood

Oral traditions and stories passed down from generation to generation form part of our history and are also part of the syncretized elements I referred to in chapter 1. Many women who have experienced the premature loss of their husbands, especially when they still have young kids, have referred to the importance of this time-honored tradition.

Spending time with family conversing about the family history is seriously one of the best ways that children not only learn values and ethics from their parents but also learn to keep traditions and memories alive. In addition, it is an opportunity to pass on stories of resilience and courage in families from past examples of our ancestors. These stories of courage and resilience also foster grit and determination. Such stories therefore have a big impact on achieving holistic wealth.

Children who spend quality time with their loved ones have more self-confidence. They are more sociable and have higher self-esteem because they sense that their parents value them. Also, kids with self-esteem find it easy to build relationships.

Children and adolescents who spend more time with their parents are less likely to experiment with substances like cigarettes, alcohol, and marijuana. According to studies done by the National Center on Addiction and Substance Abuse via Arizona State University, teens who have infrequent family dinners are twice as likely to use tobacco, nearly twice as likely to use alcohol, and one and a half times more likely to use marijuana.

Family also benefits our elders. Research has shown that family time has profound benefits. Six years of research compiled by scientists at the University of California proves that loneliness predicts death. The study focused on 1,600 elderly participants. It revealed that of the seniors who died, 14 percent had regular visitors. In contrast, 23 percent had no family or friends who came by to see them.

MAKE THE HOLIDAYS COUNT

Holidays can be a time of renewal and also of making an impact on the lives of those less fortunate and those who have suffered tragedy and loss. The first Christmas after my husband died was spent with family and friends in New York City. The kids were able to spend time with their cousins, and despite the grief, we were able to get out and enjoy the city.

Many people volunteer or donate gifts for children in need during the holiday season. Whatever you choose, make someone else smile during the emotionally fraught time. Holidays well spent are part of a life of holistic wealth, because the holidays are one of the few times of the year when we get to reconnect with loved ones and share our lives with others. I reached out to several people to see how they make the holidays count:

USE YOUR SKILLS TO HELP OTHERS

Dr. Rubina Tahir, board-certified chiropractor, states, "I make the holidays count by using what skills I have to give to others. As a chiropractor, I offer free treatments to patients in need during the last two weeks of December. Self-care is so important when dealing with stress that I really believe it is the best way to make an impact to those less fortunate. I encourage small business owners to do the same in what capacity they have."

APPROACH HOLIDAYS AS IF THEY WERE YOUR LAST

Kelly Kandra Hughes, who has a PhD in psychology from the University of North Carolina at Chapel Hill and is a former associate professor at Benedictine University, says, "It was my desire to live a more joyful and meaningful life that prompted me to quit my job (giving up tenure, benefits, and a matching retirement plan), give up ninety-five percent of my belongings, and adopt a minimalist lifestyle. I have never been happier or healthier. My biggest piece of advice is one that I believe is often overlooked—approach the holidays as if they would be your last. As you may know, this practice is referred to as a 'death meditation,' and I believe it is essential for anyone who wants to make their day-to-day lives count."

TAKE A BREAK FROM SOCIAL MEDIA

In the interview I did with Carl Ashfield, he stated that "to really make the holiday count, I found that it was necessary to leave all mobile devices, laptops, and tablets switched off for the remainder of the holiday. I went away last year, and as bad as it sounds, I was constantly on my phone checking Facebook, Instagram, and Twitter. I promised my partner that the next time we went away, I would leave everything switched off and only use it if ever an emergency occurred. Finally, on our most recent holiday, I managed to fully concentrate on my partner and kids, and we had the most exciting holiday in a long while, as I had no distractions."

Holistic wealth includes making the holidays count, because it is through the holidays that we often reconnect with those who are most important to us. Our social relationships form part of holistic wealth, and the holiday season is when we give the best of ourselves, by giving gifts and acts of kindness to others. The Laws of Reciprocity and Abundance are fully activated during the holidays, because it is also a time when we get to reflect on our lives and make resolutions and goals to start afresh. As a result, the holidays, especially Christmas and New Year's, present that critical period of transition, from one year to the next and from one season of growth to the other.

34

MARRIAGE (IT'S A BEAUTIFUL THING)

What is the strangeness that unites two minds,
Disparate, contrapuntal, female, male,
That never thought such beings of two kinds
Could join, like ships that on the ocean sail
And meet and cross, as though predestinate,
When all the spacious oceans intervene
And yet their forms must coalesce and mate
Making a marriage where no match was seen?
For of your form there is some entity
Which draws from me that equal opposite
Which only longs to go where you might be
And cannot live unless you sanction it.
All of the you in me is of this sort.
That where I am you are the living heart.

—William Shakespeare, "Sonnet XII"

That night in the hospital, I prayed to God to save my husband. In effect, I was also praying to God to save my marriage. He didn't save it—in an instant it was gone. Marriage represents the impetus and nucleus for the passing on of the syncretized elements that form our genetic makeup (as I mentioned in chapter 1).

In this life, love is everything. It can heal; it can build bridges; it can end wars. Love is something that firmly grounds us in the present. I don't know if you can get more mindful than when you are in a state of being in love. If grief is the presence of love without a place to go, then being in love is the presence of mutually reciprocated love that is all encompassing and grabs the attention of every atom of your being. It captures all our senses, and everything comes to a screeching halt. The world slows down, and we are in a state of bliss. It hijacks our thoughts and impulses. Love is like a cocoon—like a coconut shell with the outer hardened husk that protects us from all external harms because of its high resistance to abrasion and the soft white inside core, full of flesh that envelops us with its softened, fragrant nutrients. I am not saying we need to be in love to feel grounded. However, love is the foremost emotion of humanity and the mother of all emotional beginnings. It goes back to Genesis in the Bible, and the beginning of the world. It encompasses the heart and soul of the six laws: Purpose, Abundance, Reciprocity, Continuous Learning, Natural Harmony and Balance, and Spiritual Self-Renewal. Love is the mother of humanity and the forbearer of everything good. Love is at the epicenter of holistic wealth.

Remember the toxic naysayers in chapter 2? Well, they also said things about how second marriages were worse than first marriages, and that I would never find anyone else like my first husband. The list went on and on. Regarding remarriage, it was mostly negative. A true gift came when Garfield's mom called to tell me that at thirty-one, I was too young to be alone—that I should find someone to share my life with. The tears welled up in my heart, in my soul, and in my eyes. She also said the boys would need someone—a father figure in their lives.

During this time, a childhood friend would call to check up on me from time to time. We were next-door neighbors as children and close family friends. From as far back as I can remember my childhood, it included him. We have been friends since about age four, but at the time I lost my husband, we lived on two separate continents, separated by vast oceans. He was in the Cayman Islands, and I was in Canada. It had seemed unlikely that we would reunite. As the opening epigraph to this chapter states, it was a "strangeness that unites two minds, / Disparate, contrapuntal, female, male, / That never thought such beings of two kinds / Could join, like ships that on the ocean sail / And meet and cross, as though predestinate."

He had never been married, and I didn't know that he had had a crush on me ever since we were kids. The rest, they say, is history: I remarried and had a little girl, Ella Alexia Blair. Garfield's mom also met him and gave her stamp of approval—and called him "her son." The baby girl was the gift my son Matthew and I had dreamed of even after Garfield's death. Matthew wanted a little sister so badly and daydreamed about it so much, the teachers called me into the school to talk about it. Matthew was the one who named his sister Ella.

I still think weddings are the most beautiful events. My husband is Lindsay Blair, and he films weddings for a living, after a long career in television and film, first working as a TV director at the Cayman Islands Television Network, then working on Emmy Award–nominated shows such as *Penn & Teller: Fool Us* and *Awesome Adventures*. He runs Blair Global Media (www.blairglobalmedia.ca), and when he comes home with footage from these lovely weddings, I am in awe at the sight of love shown by these couples.

Rabbi Shlomo Slatkin is a licensed clinical professional counselor who founded the Marriage Restoration Project, a global initiative to help keep couples together and happy, and in an interview with me he stated, "A marriage is your most powerful and deepest human relationship you can have. Your spouse is your other half, your life partner, your soul mate. They are there for you in good times and challenging times. They are your rock and a source of support, [so] that no matter what you are going through, you can always count on your spouse to be by your side and hold your hand. That's why marriage is particularly beautiful after a loss, because you still have the encouragement that your biggest cheerleader is there for you, being a source of support and meeting your needs, giving you the encouragement to get through the difficult times."

LOVE AFTER A TIME OF LOSS

Love after a time of loss can be a beautiful thing: it brings a new perspective, it decreases loneliness and increases companionship, and, for these reasons, it increases holistic wealth. Wade Brill, a lifestyle and mindfulness coach, told me in an interview that she had gotten married two months before we talked, and her wedding was the first family celebration and happy gathering after her mother passed away from cancer in 2010. She says, "At the same time, I was facing my own cancer battle. Getting married and sharing the experience with family and friends was this huge life milestone that I was able to say I survived and made it to this chapter in my life. It was an opportunity to build happy, loving memories with my family instead of focusing on the fact my mother was not present." Having opportunities to celebrate and focus on the good and on the beauty in life is so important, because we will never get those moments or opportunities back. Marriage becomes a symbolic reminder of how life continues to unfold. A reminder that with death, there is also life.

Carolyn Miller Parr, family mediator and author of *Love's Way: Living Peacefully with Your Family as Your Parents Age*, was widowed after a fifty-six-year marriage and then remarried a year and a half later. She says, "My current husband, Jim, was a widower whose wife died of cancer. They were married forty-nine years. We both knew how to be happily married, and how to be alone. Together is better. Jim and I knew each other for fifty years, because he and my first husband had worked together. That made it easy to trust one another and eliminated the need for a long courtship. We lived together for a few months. We decided to marry for several reasons: we wanted the stability of a legal commitment, we wanted to publicly seek the support of our adult children and our friends, and we wanted our relationship to be blessed by our churches."

HEALTH BENEFITS OF A GOOD MARRIAGE

The health benefits of a good marriage are well documented. A recent study published in the *Journal of Neurology, Neurosurgery and Psychiatry*[33] revealed that marriage reduces your risk of dementia, which is the seventh leading cause of death worldwide. According to the World Health Organization, about forty-seven million people around the world have the disease, and there are nearly ten million new cases every year.

Tina B. Tessina, PhD (a.k.a. "Dr. Romance") is a psychotherapist and author of *How to Be Happy Partners: Working It Out Together*. In our interview, Tina told me that "a good

---

33. Andrew Sommerlad et al., "Marriage and Risk of Dementia: Systematic Review and Meta-Analysis of Observational Studies," *Journal of Neurology, Neurosurgery and Psychiatry* 89, Issue 3, 2017, https://jnnp.bmj.com/content/89/3/231.

marriage is a blessing. There are many health benefits to a happy relationship. First, it's obviously good to have someone around who cares for you in case you become ill, have an accident, or suffer loss. Second, research shows . . . that a successful relationship is supportive, calming, and reduces stress—with corresponding health benefits such as lowered blood pressure and heightened immune response. Third, a loving partner is fun to be around, which helps reduce stress and loneliness. Fourth, partners tend to influence each other to do healthy things: exercise, eat better, have medical and dental checkups, and socialize."

As Steven Dziedzic, founder of Lasting, the marriage counseling company and the number one marriage counseling app in America, says, "Experiencing love again and again in a relationship does remarkable things to yourself and the world around you. Namely, you become a better person—because love is shaping you—and the people around you become better, too, as a result. That's the most beautiful thing this world has to offer."

Since love is at the epicenter of holistic wealth, I want to end this book with a wish of love to you. This book started with grief and, fittingly, ends with love. When you think of *Holistic Wealth*—and enact the Holistic Wealth Method in your life—think of love. I wish you love, joy, happiness, and holistic wealth in every aspect of your life.

BUILD YOUR RELATIONSHIP ASSET PORTFOLIO

In Part IV, I shared seven life lessons to build your holistic wealth in the area of your relationships and giving back:

1. Service to Others (over the Highest-Paid Position)
2. Mentorship
3. The Gift of Help
4. Relationships with the Right People
5. A Platform That Represents You
6. Time Spent with Family, and Holidays That Count
7. Marriage (It's a Beautiful Thing)

Below are six actions you can take to increase your holistic wealth in the area of relationships and giving back, such as service to others, enacting the gift of help, mentorship, and spending time with family and friends during the holidays and in your most significant relationships. Some of the items on the list are simply questions for reflection. Know that reaching outward and connecting with others while using your talents and gifts to drive humanity forward are the first steps of building a relationship asset portfolio. Choose to do one, some, or all of the following:

1. How can you serve humanity through your current endeavors? Make a list of extra ways you can do so.
2. Has mentorship impacted your life? Can you think of a way to give back through mentorship?
3. How can you help others to enrich their holistic wealth bank accounts? Think of two ways you can help others to do this.
4. Write down ways in which you can take steps to network more with others.
5. Think about ways to make the holidays count.
6. If you're married or in a relationship, hug your spouse or significant other. Make a commitment to enrich your relationship or marriage more and more each day.

PART V

APPLYING HOLISTIC WEALTH

35

THE HOLISTIC WEALTH PORTFOLIO™

The Holistic Wealth Portfolio is critical to preparing for recovery from disruption. It comprises relationships and giving, life purpose, physical health and spiritual health, and financial independence—all building blocks of holistic wealth. When I think of a life well lived I think about these four key building blocks. When designing a Holistic Wealth Portfolio, it's important to honestly assess these building blocks and to think of areas where there's the most need. A Holistic Wealth Portfolio can be for a team or an organization, or it can be personal to each individual.

When people identify what a life well lived means for them (chapter 1), identify their goals with wisdom (chapter 4), and think carefully about financial planning and independence (chapters 12 through 18), they start to see how these concepts work together. The pandemic has given people food for thought as to what we all really value. People are starting to redefine what success means to them. We're starting to think about the parts of our pandemic lives that we want to take into our post-pandemic future. People are starting to redefine success on their own terms. Workers are no longer interested in defining themselves by a standard that's outdated and archaic.

What we're seeing is a shift toward holistic wealth—a life based on a more fulfilling, sustainable definition of success, which also includes well-being, being able to tap into inner peace and joy, and having the time to engage in more meaningful experiences.

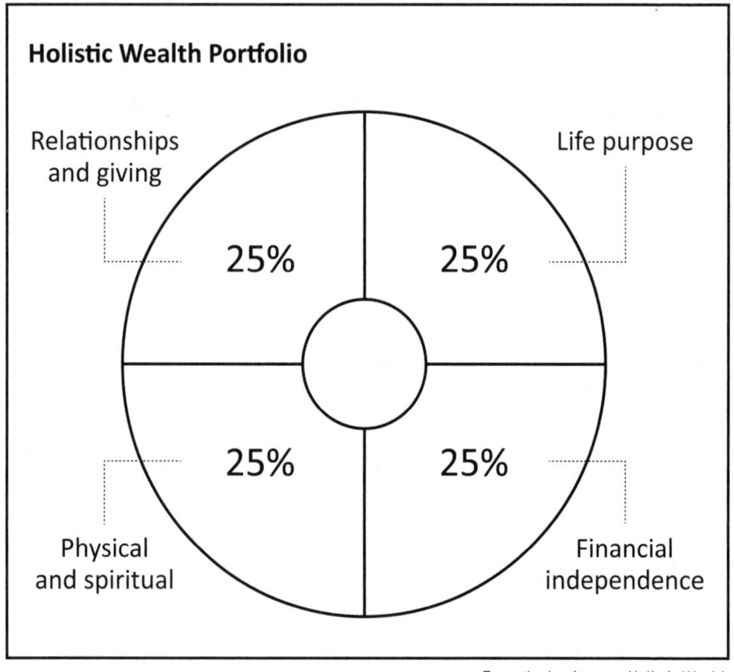

From the Institute on Holistic Wealth

If you need help designing your own personal Holistic Wealth Portfolio, or one for your organization or team, contact us at the Institute on Holistic Wealth. A portfolio approach to this framework helps individuals, teams, and organizations spot weaknesses in different areas, as well as areas for improvement.

ORGANIZATIONS AND HOLISTIC WEALTH

The concept of holistic wealth can be used within organizations by expanding the triple-bottom-line concept that took hold in the late 1990s. That concept includes social (employee) impacts, economic/financial impacts, and environmental impacts. The Holistic Wealth Development Index outlined at the end of this book (see chapter 36) can also help organizations assess their actions and decisions. Applying a holistic wealth lens to our decision-making is critical going forward. Ideally, every organization should have trained Certified Holistic Wealth™ Consultants embedded into teams and employee resource groups. In addition, every organization would benefit from having Holistic Wealth Project Groups, which would be comprised of groups or employees in each region who are energized and motivated to help each other achieve holistic wealth both at work and in their personal lives, and therefore drive organizational purpose, resilience, innovation, wellness, and success.

36

THE HOLISTIC WEALTH DEVELOPMENT INDEX™

This index contains a modern framework that allows people to renew themselves and to develop resilience in the face of disruption and setbacks. As a result, it encompasses a model for societal and individual resilience, as part of the art of recovery from disruption, that is also necessary for growth. It provides a framework for applying a holistic wealth lens to our decision-making. It takes into consideration the necessary supports that are required for individuals to be able to achieve holistic wealth—even in the face of adversity, tragedy, and setbacks. Given that we all face these types of setbacks, a society or organization that is able to fully support individuals to help them bounce back quickly and still achieve their fullest potential in life will be ahead of the curve in developing its human capital to its fullest. A more resilient society is a more prosperous and successful—and holistically wealthy—society. The Holistic Wealth Development approach is the counter theory we need in a time of urgent human problems and economic and social inequality. The Holistic Wealth Development Index is different from other approaches such as the Human Development reports put forward by the United Nations Development Programme, as well as by other pioneers such as Martha Nussbaum in her book *Creating Capabilities: The Human Development Approach.* The Holistic Wealth Development Index is an approach centered in creating resilience after bouncing back from life-changing setbacks, which we all face at some point in life, but it also entails a comparative quality-of-life assessment. My approach is preoccupied not only with the Nussbaumian question of what a person is able to do and become in life but also with how it is possible for a person to bounce back from life-altering setbacks, and how society enables that for the good of all [hu]mankind. It is therefore entrenched in the need for social justice and economic equality. Its central goal is to improve the quality of life for all people and to foster economic and social resilience and holistic wealth. In an era of #MeToo and activism around gender rights, it also presents a more modern framework to engender rights and freedoms. Women can't access holistic wealth if they are humiliated and lose their dignity when speaking out against sexual harassment or domestic violence. Parents with children can't access holistic wealth if, after returning to work from paid maternity, paternity, or other types of unpaid leave, their careers stagnate, since that stagnation could lead to poverty. In a modern society, there is still no form of recognition for the work of child-caregiving in the home.

My approach also entails a list of holistic wealth functionalities—and the idea that societies that embrace holistic wealth for all embrace these opportunities for individuals without humiliation and loss of dignity. This approach also acknowledges the principle of the "Hiding Hand," which holds that life-altering setbacks can take place at any time in the life course and that individuals need to be empowered to be resilient to overcome these setbacks in order to be able to contribute to society to their fullest potential.

For instance, after chronic illness, widowhood, or divorce at an early age, a young woman with young children may have to choose between a career and affordable childcare for her children, and if she has to choose the latter, she is then cut off from career advancement and salary progression, which robs her of basic dignity. This is an example of a choice against holistic wealth that people face on a daily basis. Another tragic choice that is pervasive in many societies is choosing between leisure time and earning a decent living—thus creating widescale mental health issues. A third tragic choice that is related to the first one above is that of the young widow who eventually goes back into the workforce after her childcare duties and is seen as having skills that have atrophied and therefore given meaningless work (or worse, demoted), which stifles her career progression, harms her ability to earn more money to take care of her kids, and robs her of her dignity. If you recall, *dignity* is a contributor to holistic wealth. All of these choices have holistic wealth ripple effects on other aspects of our lives.

TEN COMPONENTS OF THE HOLISTIC WEALTH DEVELOPMENT INDEX

1. **Life, Well Lived:** This includes not only living to the end of a human life span, and not dying prematurely, but also being able to live a life well lived. Being able to pursue life passions and hobbies and being able to take breaks to explore other interests.
2. **Life on One's Terms:** Being able to have a voice and the freedom to speak up against sexual harassment, racial discrimination, discrimination

based on sexual orientation, and domestic violence without fear of recrimination and loss of dignity.

3. **The Natural World:** Being able to live in harmony with nature and animals, plants, and biodiversity. This includes being able to assert individual freedoms in helping to address great environmental challenges of our time such as climate change and ocean pollution.
4. **Lifelong Learning (Education for the Fourth Industrial Revolution):** Being able to fully participate in the future of work—through building resilience throughout the life course, such as learning skills to enable success in vague and constantly changing environments and emphasizing soft skills. Being able to acquire skills in a variety of ways including mentorships—including lateral and reverse mentorships that foster holistic wealth.
5. **A Well-Planned Future:** Being able to access supports and services to have a well-planned future. This includes retirement planning and counseling on having a future that is intentionally designed.
6. **A Financially Secure Future (Plan for Longevity):** Being able to build a financially secure future through a mix of accessible public pensions that are adequate and provide for a certain threshold of income during retirement. Being able to access gainful employment, should an individual choose to work after retirement. This also includes being able to access financial advice through the life span as well as accessing financial

literacy initiatives throughout the life course to enable financial planning.

7. **Physical Health:** Being able to access physical supports and services. This includes nutrition supports as well as services for those with very rare diseases and disorders. This also includes supports for mental health, for cradle-to-the-grave mental health services.
8. **Physical Nourishment:** Being able to access a nutritional safety net, clean water, proper sanitary conditions, and other wellness supports.
9. **Leisure Time and Hobbies:** Being able to access leisure activities and opportunities for hobbies and learning skills, channeling creative pursuits to build resilience, and increasing social relationships. This also includes being able to access time off to renew after a setback and to have supports for successful reintegration back into the workplace.
10. **Control over One's Time and Environment:**
    - Physical assets: being able to own land, a home, and leave an inheritance.
    - Inclusive technology and thriving in a digital age: being able to access the latest technology; leveraging technology for diversity and inclusion and for full access and participation in the economy and labor force for all.
    - Privacy and protection of individual data: being able to have control over one's personal information on online platforms such as social media. Protection from online predators and online hate and abuse.

SUMMARY AND CONCLUSION

Tragedy and setbacks have a way of guiding us to our true passions and purpose in life. Perhaps it's a physical torque, like a bolt of lightning from the universe edging us onto a path we were meant for. What I know for sure is that each one of us was created uniquely to manifest a special purpose in life. I also know that if we seek our purpose and achieve it, holistic wealth is guaranteed. We are made up of billions of atoms. Each atom has a center called a nucleus. The nucleus is made up of tiny parts, or particles. These are called protons and neutrons. Circling the nucleus are more particles. These are electrons. Each electron has an electrical charge. They jump from atom to atom to create an electrical current. These electrons and atoms are the fire that lights us! When we veer off our purpose, the electrical charges burst into being and try to channel us back on that path. If we are receptive and stop to actually notice, we can get back on a path to achieving our purpose and holistic wealth.

Each of these laws that govern holistic wealth are part of the gift of the universe. The Laws of Abundance, Reciprocity, Natural Harmony and Balance, Spiritual Self-Renewal, Purpose (and Service to Humanity), and Continuous Learning are governed by the universe. If you put them into practice, you can achieve whatever it is you have always dreamed about.

A good way of remembering these laws is to set aside a day per week for each one. Start in the order in which they appear in this book, as illustrated below, and set aside time each day to practice.

1. Law #1: The Law of Abundance
2. Law #2: Spiritual Self-Renewal, which is broken down into four components
3. Law #3: Purpose in Life (Service to Humanity)
4. Law #4: The Law of Reciprocity—give and you will receive
5. Law #5: The Law of Natural Harmony and Balance
6. Law #6: The Law of Continuous Learning

ACKNOWLEDGMENTS

To Matthew and Alexander Mullings, who lost a father and gained another one in the process, I love you dearly; thanks for walking this journey with me. To Ella, my little girl who came a few years later but lit up my life like a candle on fire—thank you. To Lindsay, my dear husband and the biggest supporter of my writing, producer of the *Holistic Wealth* podcast, thank you.

To my mom, Dr. Bernice Williams, you are my rock and strength; thank you so much for your support of this edition of the book and actually encouraging me every step of the way to get this done (thanks for being my accountability partner). Thank you for coauthoring with me the Holistic Healing online course now delivered through the Institute on Holistic Wealth. To my dad, Oliver Williams, for your support through those long months after Garfield's death and during COVID-19—thank you. To Kelly Rutherford, author of the foreword of this edition, thank you for your support and your amazing words and insights—you are truly a gift to us all. To the trailblazers and experts quoted in this book, thank you for your wisdom and insights.

To my amazing Certified Holistic Wealth™ Consultants who drove this movement forward and encouraged me to create the Certified Holistic Wealth™ Consultant Program, in the midst of a pandemic, including Alison Setton (First

Consultant), Paige Brettle, Dr. Deana Stevenson, and many others, you all inspire me, more than words can express.

To the team at Girl Friday Productions, including Ingrid Emerick, Emilie Sandoz-Voyer, Tiffany Taing, Paul Barrett, Georgie Hockett, and Micah Schmidt, thank you for your support and your help in getting this book out in the world in excellent form.

Thank you to the various editors and publishers who gave me a platform to share my writing and experiences, such as Arianna Huffington, and the editors at *FinerMinds* (Mindvalley), who allowed me to write alongside some of the great motivational writers such as T. Harv Eker and Vishen Lakhiani. To Merin Curotto, former executive editor of the *New York Observer,* who championed the viral article and allowed me to become a contributor to the *Observer,* thank you. To Rob Carrick, who featured the article in the *Globe and Mail,* thank you. To Claire McIntosh, editor-in-chief of Sisters From AARP, thank you.

To the readers on Aspire-Canada, KeishaBlair.com, and the Modern Widow—thank you.

BIBLIOGRAPHY

Allen, Summer. *The Science of Awe* (a white paper prepared for the John Templeton Foundation by the Greater Good Science Center at UC Berkeley). September 2018.

Anderson, Craig, Maria Monroy, and Dacher Keltner. "Awe in Nature Heals: Evidence from Military Veterans, At-Risk Youth, and College Students." *Emotion* 18, no. 8 (December 2018): 1195–1202.

Aristotle. *Politica*, Book 1, parts I–II, 1127–1130.

Buber, Martin. *I and Thou*. Scribner (Classic edition), June 13, 2000.

Carlson, Kristi. *Eat Like a Gilmore: The Unofficial Cookbook for Fans of Gilmore Girls*. Skyhorse Publishing, 2016.

Chopra, Deepak. *The Seven Spiritual Laws of Success: A Practical Guide to the Fulfillment of Your Dreams*. San Rafael: New World Library and Amber-Allen Publishing, 1994.

Dudley, Chris. "Money Lessons Learned from Pro Athletes' Financial Fouls." CNBC online, May 14, 2018, https://www.cnbc.com/2018/05/14/money-lessons-learned-from-pro-athletes-financial-fouls.html.

Dweck, Carol S. *Mindset: The New Psychology of Success.* New York: Ballantine Books, 2008.

Ellis, Kristina. *Confessions of a Scholarship Winner: The Secrets That Helped Me Win $500,000 in Free Money for College. How You Can Too*. Worthy Books, 2013.

Emerson, Richard. "Power-Dependence Relations." *American Sociological Review* 27, no. 1 (February 1962): 31–41.

Ferriss, Tim. *Tools of Titans: The Tactics, Routines, and*

Habits of Billionaires, Icons, and World-Class Performers. Houghton Mifflin Harcourt, 2016.

Foss, Kimberly. *Wealthy by Design: A 5-Step Plan for Financial Security.* Austin: Greenleaf Book Press, 2013.

Frankl, Victor. *Man's Search for Meaning.* New York: Pocketbooks, 1959.

Gallo, Amy. *HBR Guide to Dealing with Conflict* (HBR Guide Series). Harvard Business Review Press. April 4, 2017.

Gallo, Amy. "What to Do When a Personal Crisis Is Hurting Your Professional Life." *Harvard Business Review,* November 2017.

Ganz, Marshall. *Why David Sometimes Wins: Leadership, Organization, and Strategy in the California Farm Worker Movement.* New York: Oxford University Press, 2009.

Ganz, Marshall. "People, Power and Change." Lecture/ classroom organizing notes, John F. Kennedy School of Government, Harvard University, Cambridge, Massachusetts, spring 2018.

Gilbert, Elizabeth. *Eat Pray Love: One Woman's Search for Everything Across Italy, India and Indonesia.* Viking Penguin, 2006.

Gladwell, Malcolm. "Six Degrees of Lois Weisberg." *New Yorker,* January 11, 1999, 52–63.

Gladwell, Malcolm. *The Tipping Point: How Little Things Can Make a Big Difference.* Back Bay Books, 2002.

Gould, Stephen Jay. *Time's Arrow, Time's Cycle: Myth and Metaphor in the Discovery of Geological Time.* Cambridge: Harvard University Press, 1987.

Graham, Benjamin. *The Intelligent Investor: The Definitive Book on Value Investing,* rev. ed. New York: HarperBusiness, 2006.

Graham, Benjamin, and David Dodd. *Security Analysis,* 6th ed. New York: McGraw-Hill Education, 2008.

Granovetter, Mark. *Getting a Job: A Study of Contacts and*

Careers, 2nd ed. Chicago: University of Chicago Press, 2018.

Halliwell, Ed. *Into the Heart of Mindfulness: Finding a Way of Well-Being*. Platkus Books, 2016.

Hammond, Keli. *Craved: The Secret Sauce to Building a Highly-Successful, Standout Brand*. B Classic LLC, 2019.

Hanson, Rick. *Hardwiring Happiness: The New Brain Science of Contentment, Calm, and Confidence*. New York: Harmony Books, 2013.

Hatmaker, Jen. *Of Mess and Moxie: Wrangling Delight Out of This Wild and Glorious Life*. Nashville: Thomas Nelson, 2017.

Higuera, Valencia, "Poll Finds Salary Alone Won't Make You Wealthy." GOBankingRates, June 29, 2017, https://www.gobankingrates.com/making-money/wealth/heres-salary-alone-never-make-super-wealthy/.

Hirschman, Albert O. "The Principle of the Hiding Hand." National Affairs Inc. and the American Enterprise Institute, Winter 1967.

Jay, Meg. *The Defining Decade: Why Your Twenties Matter—And How to Make the Most of Them Now*. Little, Brown & Company, 2015.

Johnson, Robert, Thomas Robinson, and Stephen Horan. *Strategic Value Investing: Practical Techniques of Leading Value Investors*. New York: McGraw-Hill Education, 2013.

Jones, Bill T. *Last Night on Earth*. New York: Pantheon Books, 1995.

Kenyon, Mary Potter. *Coupon Crazy: The Science, Savings, and Stories Behind America's Extreme Obsession*. Familius, 2013.

Kenyon, Mary Potter. *Refined by Fire: A Journey of Grief and Grace*. Familius, 2014.

Kerpen, Dave. *The Art of People: 11 Simple People Skills that Will Get You Everything You Want*. New York: Penguin Random House, 2016.

Kierkegaard, S. *Parables of Kierkegaard*. Edited by Thomas C. Oden. Princeton: Princeton University Press, 1989. Originally published in 1845 (translated by David F. Swenson in 1941).

Lamott, Anne. *Bird by Bird: Some Instructions on Writing and Life*. New York: Anchor Books, 1995.

Langer, Ellen. "Mindful Learning." *Current Directions in Psychological Science* 9, no. 6. (December 2000).

Langer, Ellen. *Mindfulness*, 25th anniversary ed. Da Capo Lifelong Books, 2014.

Lewis, C. S. *A Grief, Observed*. New York: HarperCollins, 2007.

Lewis, C. S. *Surprised by Joy: The Shape of My Early Life*. New York: HarperCollins, 2017.

Lloyd, Peter. "No Matter How Much Money You Have You Are NEVER Happy: Even Millionaires Say They Need to at Least Double Their Wealth to Be Truly Content, First Study of Its Kind Finds." DailyMail.com, December 2018, https://www.dailymail.co.uk/sciencetech/article-6466731/Money-doesnt-buy-happiness-Millionaires-say-need-double-wealth-happy.html.

Matthews, Sue. *Paint Your Hair Blue: A Celebration of Life with Hope for Tomorrow in the Face of Pediatric Cancer*. Morgan James Publishing, 2018.

Morin, Amy. *13 Things Mentally Strong People Don't Do: Take Back Your Power, Embrace Change, Face Your Fears, and Train Your Brain for Happiness and Success*. New York: William Morrow Paperbacks, 2017.

Nussbaum, Martha. *Creating Capabilities: The Human Development Approach*. Harvard University Press, 2011.

Parr, Carolyn Miller. *Love's Way: Living Peacefully with Your Family as Your Parents Age*. Peabody: Hendrickson Publishers, 2019.

Saltz, Gail. *The Power of Different: The Link Between Disorder and Genius*. New York: Flatiron Books, 2018.

Santana, Alan. *Unprotected*. Page Publishing, 2017.

Seligman, Martin. *Flourish: A Visionary New Understanding of Happiness and Well-Being*. Atria Books, 2012.

Seneca, Lucius. "On the Shortness of Life." Translated by John W. Basore, Loeb Classical Library. London: William Heinemann, 1932, http://www.forumromanum.org/literature/seneca_younger/brev_e.html.

Shumsky, Susan. *Awaken Your Divine Intuition: Receive Wisdom, Blessings, and Love by Connecting with Spirit*. Weiser, 2016.

Shumsky, Susan. *Awaken Your Third Eye: How Accessing Your Sixth Sense Can Help You Find Knowledge, Illumination, and Intuition*. Weiser, 2015.

Shumsky, Susan. *Divine Revelation*. Touchstone, 1996.

Smith, Adam. *The Wealth of Nations*. New York, NY: Bantam Classic, 1776.

Sommerlad, Andrew, Josh Ruegger, Archana Singh-Manoux, Glyn Lewis, and Gill Livingston. "Marriage and Risk of Dementia: Systematic Review and Meta-Analysis of Observational Studies." *Journal of Neurology, Neurosurgery and Psychiatry* 89, Issue 3, 2017, https://jnnp.bmj.com/content/89/3/231.

Strayed, Cheryl. *Wild: From Lost to Found on the Pacific Crest Trail*. New York: Alfred A. Knopf, 2012.

Tessina, Tina. *How to Be Happy Partners: Working It Out Together*. Create Space, 2016.

Thomas, Rachel, Marianne Cooper, Ellen Konar, et al. *Women in the Workplace 2018*. Study published by McKinsey & Company and Leanin.org.

Toterhi, Tim. *The HR Guide to Getting and Crushing Your Dream Job*. Plotline Leadership, 2018.

Ware, Bronnie. *The Top Five Regrets of the Dying: A Life Transformed by the Dearly Departing*. Bolinda Publishing Pty Ltd, 2017.

ABOUT THE AUTHOR

Keisha Blair is the award-winning, bestselling author of *Holistic Wealth: 32 Life Lessons to Help You Find Purpose, Prosperity, and Happiness* and the *Holistic Wealth Personal Workbook*. She is widely regarded as the "Mother of Holistic Wealth," and is founder of the Holistic Wealth Movement and the Institute on Holistic Wealth. She has been profiled in the *New York Times, Forbes,* the *Harvard Business Review, Essence* magazine, and many other publications. Her book *Holistic Wealth* has been well received by highly influential TV audiences such as the producers of Jada Pinkett Smith's *Red Table Talk* and the producers of *The Mel Robbins Show* (some of whom were formerly of Oprah's Favorite Things), as well as Yahoo Finance's Final Round. She was part of the Canadian prime minister's supporting delegation to the World Economic Forum in 2018 as well as the East-Asia (ASEAN) Summit in Singapore. Her viral article, "My Husband Died at Age 34; Here Are 40 Life Lessons I Learned from It," originally published on *Thrive Global*'s website, was featured on or linked to by over 160 websites and viewed by over fifty million people worldwide. She is a trained economist and also a graduate of the Executive Leadership Program at Harvard University's John F. Kennedy School of Government. She is the founder of several nonprofit initiatives, including Aspire-Canada (as well as the

Aspire-Canada memorial scholarship). She is the host of the Holistic Wealth segment on the award-winning, internationally syndicated *Daily Flash* TV show, and hosts the *Holistic Wealth* podcast. She lives in Ottawa, Ontario, with her family.

JOIN THE HOLISTIC WEALTH MOVEMENT

Here are ways you can join the Holistic Wealth Movement and impact the lives of others:

- **Become a Certified Holistic Wealth™ Consultant** with the Keisha Blair Institute on Holistic Wealth (visit the website at www.instituteonholisticwealth.com).
- **Access the *Holistic Wealth Employee Benefits Tool*:** Work-life integration is the key to women's and parents' success at work. The concept of holistic wealth has been operationalized into an actionable video series that will help employees integrate holistic wealth at work, to improve their mental health, productivity, and focus. Employers can learn more about how to access this course for their employees by emailing info@keishablair.com.
- **Consider a Brand or Nonprofit Partnership:** Interested in partnering with the Institute on Holistic Wealth to create a consumer offering or campaign? Please send an email to info@keishablair.com.
- **Become a member of the Institute on Holistic Wealth:** Visit the Institute on Holistic Wealth website at https://www.instituteonholisticwealth.com/membership-levels/.

- **Subscribe to the *Holistic Wealth Podcast with Keisha Blair*** and tell a friend. If you belong to a company or organization, contact us to partner with us.
- **Start your own Holistic Wealth Project / Accountability Group** with friends, coworkers, or family members to stick to your goals and keep each other on track.
- **Leave us a review** on Amazon, Indigo, Barnes & Noble, or any platform where you are able to. When readers leave a book review, you help other readers discover the book and this great message.
- If you have a blog, website, or podcast, **share your thoughts on the book** so others can find it and benefit from this message of holistic wealth.
- **If you're interested in one-on-one coaching, or help with any of the points mentioned above,** contact me directly at info@keishablair.com.

Here's how you can connect with me:

1. Sign up for the newsletter and email me on www.KeishaBlair.com
2. Share your own stories of holistic wealth (#HolisticWealth and #HolisticWealthbook) and connect with me on Instagram and Twitter: @KeishaOBlair
3. Follow me on Facebook: https://www.facebook.com/keishablairauthor/
4. For feedback or ideas on the book or the movement on holistic wealth, you can email me at info@keishablair.com
5. Follow me on Instagram: https://www.instagram.com/keishaoblair/?hl=en

For book clubs: Please download the reading guide at www.keishablair.com to guide your book club discussions.

To take the Personal Financial Identity Quiz from the Institute on Holistic Wealth, please visit: www.instituteonholisticwealth.com/take-the-quiz/.

Find out more about preventing Adverse Childhood Experiences (ACEs) and assessing your own history of trauma here: www.cdc.gov/violenceprevention/aces/fastfact.html.

Take the ACEs quiz here: developingchild.harvard.edu/media-coverage/take-the-ace-quiz-and-learn-what-it-does-and-doesnt-mean/.